DIVING

Books by Steve Lehrman

Diving   *1978*
 (WITH SAMMY LEE, M.D.)

Figure Skating   *1978*
 (WITH DIANNE DE LEEUW)

The World of Horseback Riding   *1976*
 (WITH NEAL SHAPIRO)

Your Career in Harness Racing   *1975*

DIVING

Dr. Sammy Lee

WITH STEVE LEHRMAN

NEW YORK   1979   ATHENEUM

Library of Congress Cataloging in Publication Data

Lee, Sammy, 1920–

    Diving.

    1. Diving.   I. Lehrman, Steve, joint author.

II. Title.

GV837.L39 1978   797.2   78–55522

ISBN 0–689–10815–X

Published simultaneously in Canada by McClelland and Stewart Ltd.
Manufactured in the United States of America
Composition by Connecticut Printers, Inc., Hartford, Connecticut
Printed and bound by Fairfield Graphics, Fairfield, Pennsylvania
Designed by Kathleen Carey
First Edition

Dedication

This book is dedicated to my mother and father, who emigrated from Korea to have their children born as free Americans.

Acknowledgments

I would like to thank my sisters, Dolly and Mary, who worked with my parents so that I could use every second to study to become a physician and train to become an Olympic diving champion.

Thanks also to the late James Frederick Ryan, who taught both Dick Smith (U.S. diving coach in the 1964 and 1968 Olympic Games) and me to dive.

Thanks to my wife, Roz, and my daughter, Pamela, and son, Sammy, who shared husband and father with divers from all over the world—especially with Bob Webster, two-time Olympic gold-medal diving champion (Rome, 1960 and Tokyo, 1964), and Greg Louganis, at age sixteen the youngest male diver in Olympic history to get a silver medal (Montreal, 1976). Greg has also won the 1978 world diving title at the third World Aquatic Games, which were held in Berlin.

I would also like to thank Greg Louganis, John Lynch, and Jane Ward for their cooperation as photographic subjects.

Contents

DIVING

Introduction

FANCY DIVING IS both an art and a sport. As an art, it has the beauty and grace of ballet. As a sport, it is gymnastics performed over water. A diver is catapulted from a springboard to do twists and flips before gravity brings him down to earth, into the pool below. A diver can be likened to an astronaut. The springboard serves as his launching pad, propelling him into a proper orbit and allowing him to safely accomplish his task without fear or flaw before a safe spashdown.

Diving is a valid art form. The athlete must begin with a basic dive. He then creates his own interpretation of that move, plans it in his mind, and transforms his idea into physical action as he thrusts from the springboard.

Diving is also a most challenging sport. When entering competitions, you not only challenge yourself but other divers as well. Even though there are certain fundamentals common to all divers, no two will execute the same maneuver in the same way. The better diver wins.

The sport is quite thrilling—from the beginner's anticipation and fear when attempting a new dive to the adrenalin flowing through the body of an Olympic diver as he prepares to execute a dive he has practiced for years, hoping it is good enough to win a gold medal.

Unlike football or tennis players, divers don't get a second chance to make up for an error at a later stage of a contest. You get only one chance on each dive. There is no such thing as "defense" in the sport of diving. After a poor dive on your part, you can only hope the opposition miscues. If not, be resigned to something less than a first-place finish. For the diver, *each* dive is like serving match point, swinging with two strikes, and heading for the goal line with no time left on the scoreboard. There is no margin for error.

I've spent many years as a competitive diver and coach and have come to realize an important fact: To become a quality diver, your desire to succeed must always be greater than your fear of getting lost in learning new dives. If not, you won't make real progress and you won't succeed as a competitive diver.

Diving is not a simple sport. Years ago, as I struggled to improve, I suppose my motto was, "Disgusted, but never discouraged." I hated making mistakes but was determined to reach my goal.

It takes a lot of courage to become a diving champion.

If you have doubts, find a sport that will demand less. But if you believe you have real desire to perform to the best of your ability, to want to do the best dive you can possibly do, and to learn as many dives as you can—you have much to gain.

As in all sports, if you are serious about gaining proficiency, you must be taught by someone with a greater knowledge of the material. We hope this book will serve to stimulate your interest. Through words, pictures, and diagrams, we want to show what fun diving can be.

Proceed slowly, step-by-step. If your interest remains keen, you may want to seek out formal instruction to hone your skills. A diving camp may be a logical first step. There are many good diving camps located throughout the country, and as the United States becomes more involved in Olympic sports, the number of camps will grow.

Besides the challenge of the sport and the enjoyment and fulfillment of the art, you can also learn the value of determination and concentration. These qualities will prove a great asset to you in whatever you do for the rest of your life.

General Safety Pointers

- BEFORE MAKING *any* dive, be sure the person who preceded you into the pool has safely cleared the area.
- Never dive headfirst into any lake, ocean, or pool unless you know that the water level in the area you will be diving into is a minimum of nine feet deep when you are standing no higher than three feet off the surface.
- Never let your hands pull apart or to the side on any headfirst dive, or you will expose your head to the bottom of the pool. Lock your hands so you can do a handstand on the bottom to decrease the entry impact. Entry momentum can be lessened by bringing your knees up into a tuck position, or somersault, as your feet disappear under the water.
- Never dive with a head cold, this can cause earaches and sinusitis.

• When diving, do not turn your head to either side. The result could be a broken eardrum.

• Learn to exhale from the nostrils when diving feet-first. This will prevent water rushing up into the nose and being forced into the sinuses and possibly the ears.

• Prior to the swimming-and-diving season, check with your doctor to be sure your ear canals are clean. If ears remain wet all the time, "swimmer's ear" can result. Touching the outside of the ear and finding it tender is one symptom. This could mean that there are boils in the ear canal. The best preventive measure is to put drops of rubbing alcohol into the ear canals after swimming. A 50-50 solution of white vinegar and alcohol is also excellent. This mixture will help keep ears dry and the skin acid (alkaline skin is more susceptible to infections).

• When in doubt whether or not it is best to dive, check with your physician.

Beginning to Dive

WHEN YOU ARE preparing to dive into any nonregulation Olympic-type pool, there are several things to be done to insure a safe diving session.

Jump into the pool feetfirst, to familiarize yourself with the pool's topography. Answer these questions:

How deep is it?
How fast does the deep end become shallow?
How far out from the end of the diving board does the bottom begin to incline to the shallow end? If you dive too far out, or to the side, you could injure yourself by not expecting to strike bottom so quickly.

On an inward dive, how deep is the water directly inside of the end of the diving board?

Always be aware of the bottom of the pool. Not taking the time to check could result in an injury—anything from broken teeth or a broken nose to a broken neck. That time-worn saying, "An ounce of prevention is worth a pound of cure," is most accurate in this situation.

Always be aware that a swimmer might swim under you or that the preceding diver might not have gotten out of your flight pattern. Look before you "leap"!

FIRST TIME OFF THE BOARD

It is most important to feel comfortable when diving into the water. To begin with, dive in headfirst from the side of the pool. After you can do this, entering the water in a forward dive (or swimmer's racing dive, which is similar to a diver's belly flop), it's time to begin work on the board.

The low board (one-meter springboard) will probably seem more like ten meters in the air. Take a deep breath and go out and stand at the end of the board. Pick a spot in the water just a few feet in front of your toes and aim your hands at that spot.

Raise your arms completely straight above your head and pressing against your ears. Bend at the waist. Never

With arms over your head, lean forward and spot your entry target. Be sure not to bend knees or raise your head.

bend your knees. This will change your angle of entry as you fall, resulting in a chest- or belly-flop.

Now stretch for that spot in the water on the bottom of the pool. The spot and your hands should be in your line of vision. As you aim, just keep bending at the waist until gravity takes you into the water.

Fight the temptation to bend your knees. Don't look up by raising your head, or you will be sure to belly-flop in the pool.

As your hands strike the water's surface, tighten stomach, thigh, and leg muscles. Stretch your feet and toes and reach for the spot you are aiming for at the bottom of the pool. Always be alert—the bottom can come up quicker than you think, especially if your dive is perfect. Always be prepared to break your fall with your arms and hands instead of your head.

The one-meter Durafirm Standard Board with adjustable fulcrum.

SETTING THE BOARD

You must decide where to place the fulcrum of the diving board. The fulcrum is a bar located under the board that can be moved forward or backward. If it's moved back, the board bends more slowly and softly. If it's positioned forward, the leverage is shorter, hence the board is stiffer and quicker.

The proper setting really should depend upon each

The natural walk to the board demonstrated on a three-meter Durafirm Board with adjustable fulcrum. Note the straight position of the head and back.

diver's inherent rhythm and timing. The ideal placement of the fulcrum can be determined from a coach's experience, or from trial-and-error on the part of the diver.

Some divers like to set the board slightly tighter for back takeoffs. My advice is to keep the setting as close as possible to the one chosen for the forward approach. This makes it simpler to keep timing and rhythm constant on *all* board work.

I strongly advise against trying to set the board differently for each dive! Not only for the above reason, but also because, during a meet, you will surely lose your cool kicking the fulcrum to and fro, looking for that perfect (and I think unnecessary) specific setting.

Types of Dives

SPRINGBOARD DIVES:

GROUP I—FORWARD DIVES — Approach end of board in forward direction and dive toward the water.

GROUP II—BACKWARD DIVES — Stand backward on the board and rotate away from the board to the water.

GROUP III—REVERSE DIVES — Approach end of board in forward direction. Upon taking off, change directions and rotate toward the board while jumping a safe distance away.

GROUP IV—INWARD DIVES	Stand backward on board, rotate forward toward the board while jumping a safe distance away.
GROUP V—TWISTING DIVES	Any one of the other four types of dives combined with a twist.

Platform dives:

(Groups I–V same as above, only done from a stationary platform.)

GROUP VI—ARMSTAND DIVES	Diver balances on end of platform in a handstand, then performs a dive from that position.

The book *Rules on Competitive Diving,* published annually by the Amateur Athletic Union (A.A.U.), lists a set of rules for competitive diving in the United States. The Federation International Natation Association (F.I.N.A.) publishes its guidelines for all Olympic competitions in swimming and diving.

Each dive is classified into five groups from the springboard (whether from one meter or three meters) and six groups from the tower. The forward group consists of all dives starting from a forward approach or takeoff (that is, from the end of the diving board facing the water). The forward dive is listed as number 101 and is divided into straight, pike, tuck, and free positions.

In the straight position, the entire body is straight, with no bend at the waist or knees, and with feet together and toes pointed.

For the pike position, the body is bent at the waist and the legs must be kept straight at the knees, with the toes pointed. The pike should be as compact as possible.

In the tuck position, the body bends at the knees and hips, with feet together and toes pointed. The tuck should be as compact as possible, with the thighs and legs drawn tightly against the chest.

The free position (a combination of straight, pike, or tuck) may be used in twisting dives only as listed in the tables.

The forward group consists of sixteen dives, from the simple forward dive straight to the complex forward 3½ somersault.

Group two consists of the back dives. These are done facing the diving board, with your back to the water. Number 201 is the back dive, which is divided into straight, pike, and tuck positions.

In springboard competition, you are required to do compulsory dives: a forward dive straight, pike, or tuck; a back dive straight, pike, or tuck; a reverse dive; an inward dive; and a forward dive with a half-twist.

SCORING OF DIVES

Each dive is assigned a degree of difficulty, which has been established by a panel of diving experts. The lowest rating (1.2) belongs to the forward dive pike or tuck from the one-meter springboard. The highest rating (3.0) has been assigned to a forward 3½ somersault tuck, a back 2½ somersault tuck, and a reverse 2½ tuck from the one meter.

The required, or compulsory, dives (which every diver must perform) are:

Dive	*Degree of Difficulty*
Forward dive straight from one meter	1.4
Forward dive straight from three meters	1.6
Back dive (all positions) from one meter	1.6
Back dive (all positions) from three meters	1.7
Reverse dive straight from three meters	1.9
Reverse dive pike from three meters	1.9
Reverse dive tuck from three meters	1.7
Inward dive straight from three meters	1.6
Inward dive pike from three meters	1.3
Inward dive tuck from three meters	1.2
Forward dive half-twist straight from three meters	1.9
Forward dive half-twist pike from three meters	1.8

18

It is interesting to note that most divers feel the forward dive half-twist pike is more difficult than the same dive done from the straight (layout) position, even though the latter has a higher degree of difficulty.

In dealing with D.D. (degree of difficulty), keep in mind that on some dives, the American evaluation differs from the international standard. If you plan to become involved in diving, you would be wise to purchase the *A.A.U. Official Rule Book on Diving* each year (send $3.50 plus postage to: The A.A.U., 3400 West 86th Street, Indianapolis, Indiana 46268) and the F.I.N.A. rules every four years.

In judging dives, 10 is a perfect score. F.I.N.A. regulations set the following criteria:

Completely failed (doing only one somersault when you listed two, etc.)	0 points
Unsatisfactory	½ to 2 points
Deficient	2½ to 4½ points
Satisfactory	5 to 6 points
Good	6½ to 8 points
Very good	8½ to 10 points

A 10 means theoretical perfection, and these marks are few and far between. I've seen only a handful of dives I felt warranted 10's from all seven judges. Greg Louganis did a perfect inward 1½ pike from the ten-meter tower in the 1976 Olympic tryouts and received six 10's and one 9½. Mike Finneran received straight 10's for a back 1½ with 2½ twists in the 1972 tryouts; but I don't think that grade was deserved, since I saw his feet cross during the first twist. In my eyes, and on the scoreboard, there is a big difference between an 8½ and a 10. Just multiply 3.0 by 8½ and compare it with 3.0 by 10, and you can see the wide point spread.

In all Olympic diving contests, there are seven judges, usually one from each nation, but never one of the same nationality as the diver competing in the finals. Each judge will give his or her mark. The highest score and the lowest score will be eliminated. The five remaining awards are totalled and multiplied by the D.D., to determine the score for the dive. In contests where there are seven judges, the score is divided by five and then multiplied by three, in order to establish a score comparable to that obtained in contests where there are five judges. (A recent innovation in American competitions is the use of nine judges in the American championships, with the two highest and two lowest scores being eliminated.)

Example

Five judges (in some non-Olympic but international contests): 8, 7, 7, 7, 6½ = 21 × 2.0 = 42

Seven judges: 8, 7, 7, 7, 7, 7, 6½ = 35 × 2.0 = 70 ÷ 5 = 14 × 3 = 42

The winner of the contest is the diver with the greatest number of points. Since 1976, however, one half of the preliminary scores are added to the total final score to determine the winner.

In the preliminary competition, men divers perform eleven dives from the three-meter springboard and ten dives from the ten-meter platform. Women make ten dives from the three-meter board and eight dives from the ten-meter platform. The eight highest scorers enter the finals, where they will repeat all their dives.

Men have one optional, or voluntary, dive from the three-meter springboard, which makes it an eleven-dive contest. From the ten-meter platform, the first four compulsory dives for both men and women must not total more than 7.5 in degree of difficulty, and each dive must be from a separate group of dives. In order to be competitive, most divers total exactly 7.5. For their voluntary dives, they choose the highest degree of difficulty possible from all six categories (for men) and four out of the six groups (for women).

You don't want to give your opponent the edge, because a 0.1 variance can mean the difference between getting a gold medal or a silver, or earning a berth on a diving team or going home. On the other hand, you do not want to sacrifice or overextend your ability by selecting a dive with a high degree of difficulty on which you can earn a 4 if you don't execute it properly, when you are capable of gaining an 8 on a dive with a lesser D.D. Discretion is the better part of valor.

Getting into Diving

THE SPRINGBOARD must be used properly to get the most out of it. You must adapt your rhythm by getting the "feel" of the springboard. Stand on the end of the diving board with your toes lined up with the edge of the board and gently press your feet into the board by flexing your ankles. The board will bend. To make it bend more, rise up on your heels and push down into the board with the balls of your feet. Then permit your heels to settle down, and snap your feet and ankles into a toe stretch. Now bend your knees as the board bends, and straighten them as the board comes up. Then ankle snap to add a further downward press, which will increase the thrust of the board.

Look ahead, with arms raised and straight, just prior to raising up on toes for the downward press.

Use your arms to augment the leg motion by raising them laterally from the hips and thighs and then push downward as the feet push into the springboard. As you gain better synchronization, you will catch the rhythm of the board and soon be able to start with arms outstretched above your head in a "V" position. As your arms come down, so do the balls of your feet and your heels. Your arms provide lift by swinging forward and then back into the original "V" formation.

Now you have pressed the board down as far as you possibly can. In order to get maximum thrust, you must continue the arm swing forward and upward at the same moment the feet and ankles snap off the diving board.

Practice this body movement on the ground and see how much higher you can jump by coordinating your arms and legs. Notice how much more snap you can get from your legs when you use your arm swing correctly. Place a crossbar above your head so that you can jump upward and forward to grasp the bar; this works on the same principle as a perfect hurdle and drop into the springboard. With perfect timing, you can bend the board as far down as possible and can ride it upward to get into orbit. Note how your arms must swing into a complete circle to get that maximum jump.

Remember to lock your head and neck. Do not let your head bob, or the axis of rotation will be changed. As you springboard, keep your eyes fixed on the spot to be hit. A good dive generally should be no more than three feet from the end of the diving board, and no closer than one

The forceful downward circular throw timed with the leg push.

foot. Practice by springing off the board and landing feetfirst on forward and backward takeoffs.

The springboard is your launching pad. If used properly, it will work perfectly for you each time.

Once you are confident of the standing takeoff, the next area to concentrate on is the step-off approach, hurdle, and takeoff.

WALKING APPROACH AND TAKEOFF

The art of diving consists of the approach, the takeoff execution, and the angle of entry. Each segment must be done properly to achieve a successful dive.

APPROACH

On a forward dive, the approach is a walk or run to the end of the diving board. When reaching a point near the end of the board, the diver takes a hurdle step to spring for the dive.

The approach is begun from a stationary position on the board, at attention, with arms at your sides. Your eyes are fixed on the point at which the hurdle step will be taken, which will be at the end of the bolts, or rivets, on a Duraflex diving board. (The only boards used since 1960 are the Duraflex and Maxiflex diving boards.) The last rivet is the spot to place one's last step, or toes, to get the proper length on the hurdle. This rivet is two feet from the end of the board. Shorter divers (especially children) will have to adjust accordingly. Every spring-board and fulcrum has its own rhythm and feel. Experience and practice will enable you to adjust to each individual board.

In my time (the "good old days"), we had to move quickly across the board, because it was so stiff that motion was needed to provide momentum, not only to do the dive, but to miss the end of the board! Sometimes it was actually easier to dive off the platform. Time has progressed, and so has the quality of diving boards. The flexible boards of today require a slower approach in order to achieve maximum lift on the hurdle.

Begin your approach off either foot, and walk naturally with a slight forward lean. Each step should be of equal length. A minimum of three steps is required.

Do not watch the diving board with chin on chest.

The approach must be natural—just as natural and deliberate as if you were strolling down the street.

Ideally, each approach step is of equal length. Many novices (and even those with some experience) tend to make that last step too long. Not only will this cause a loss of balance, but it prevents attaining maximum power on the leap to the end of the diving board.

Keep in mind that three steps is the minimum. There is no maximum. Greg Louganis's five-step approach and hurdle is as comfortable and smooth for him as the four-step approach is to Olympic champion Phil Boggs. The four-step approach is one used by many divers.

Greg Louganis' perfect forward approach. Greg walks down the board in a relaxed manner, traveling in a straight line with evenly spaced steps. The pressing leg coordinates with the raising of the arms to achieve maximum lift.

Arm movement during the walk should follow natural body motion; the less swing, the better. Exaggerated arm-swinging provides added potential for loss of rhythm and balance.

On the next-to-last step prior to takeoff, your arms will instinctively swing back. As soon as you know where the pressing foot will land, your eyes should be focused at the point at the end of the board where both feet will land with the toes on the edge of the surface.

At the time of the hurdle to the takeoff point, your arms execute a hard upward swing as you step into the board. Your next-to-last step presses the board, so that the last step (on the pressing leg) pushes into the board and the hurdle leg lifts upward as forcefully as possible. As your arms rise, the knee of the hurdle leg comes up, while the toes of the pressing leg point and push you up and forward into the hurdle.

As you begin the hurdle step, do not kick your foot forward as the thigh and knee are quickly brought up to initiate the kick. A forward foot motion will throw you off-balance, since your hips will be in back of the perpendicular angle to the board necessary for a good takeoff.

At the peak of your hurdle, both arms should be fully extended over your ears in a straight line (no bend in the elbows). It is as if you were about to jump upward to grab onto a horizontal bar that was directly above your head.

Initial thrust varies with each diver's physical make-up and quickness.

The arms-and-hurdle leg raise, as the power leg's toes point to push you up and forward.

Your head should remain steady, eyes fixed on the landing site at the end of the board. As you become airborne, do not permit your chin to rest on your chest.

As your arms lift, they should be over your head at the point of hurdle. Spread your arms slightly at the jump peak and widen them into a narrow or wide "V" position. Your timing and quickness determines the width of the "V."

Your eyes are no longer focusing on the diving board, which will be seen by peripheral vision. Visual memory keeps track of foot position.

At the peak of the hurdle, your legs straighten as the toes point toward the tip of the diving board. Bring your

31

hips forward so that your entire body is perpendicular to the board. The name of the game is to get high enough on the hurdle to be in perfect balance. Your body should be completely extended, with arms stretched out, ready to press downward as the balls of your feet and your toes get into the end of the board.

As you descend on the end of the board, your arms swing downward forcefully in a circle. If your arms come too far back of your hips, you will be off-balance.

Your arms follow through in a continuous upward swing. Never bend your elbows on the press. Your back remains erect, with your head straight and neck rigid, in line with your back.

The jump landing must be with both feet together, toes at the exact end of the board, no more than a fraction of an inch away from the end of the diving board.

Stand up, reach up hard, and push off the board, without moving your head.

Helpful hints—approach

- Practice your steps while walking naturally on the ground. Have someone measure your steps. Now measure your steps while on the board. Try to match your normal walking stride.
- When starting out, it is a good idea to practice various stepoffs. Select the one most natural and effective for you. Then use it and develop it until there isn't a millimeter variation among steps on your walk to the point of hurdle. You can easily practice this every time you walk down the street.

- On a dry board, wet your feet and mark off the perfect approach. Try to mimic each step to the hurdle point.

- Those familiar with the martial arts (Kung Fu, etc.), where great amounts of power must be obtained in arm swings, all agree that the power comes from completing the circle in any arm motion. So, it stands to reason that a powerful takeoff from the diving board is better achieved when you complete the swing of the arms as you fully extend your legs, thighs, ankles, and toes in a full stretch. Make yourself as tall as you can.

- The hurdle step off one leg (similar to a long-jumper's step) must be forceful enough to clear a hurdle 1½–2 feet high over a distance of 18 inches–2½ feet.

- Height on your hurdle is important. The higher the drop into the board, the more the board flexes, and this provides greater lift in the takeoff.

- Working out on a trampoline will make it clear how the forceful downward press with the pressing leg, the synchronized downward swing of the arms, and the strong lift with the hurdle leg all combine to provide a high hurdle.

TAKEOFF

Leaving the board to become airborne must be executed with perfection, or the rest of the dive will suffer.

Be sure that your head and neck are in line with your

torso, hips, legs, and feet. Your head *must not* be angled downward. If it is, two things will happen: You will take off too soon, for the head will cause the body to lean too far out as you try to remain on the board; if you do manage to leave at a proper time, this improper position will force you to cut takeoff height and whip off the diving board. Either will result in a poor diving orbit.

On a forward dive, early takeoffs force the body out too far. On reverse dives they prevent the diver from gaining the necessary momentum. The fraction of a second it takes to lift your chin off your chest, will mean the difference between a five-point dive and a ten-point dive.

Power for the takeoff comes from the legs. They are the sole source of power. Arms provide timing and rhythm. When used properly, arms enhance the strength of the leg lift. The downward press of the arms, perfectly timed with the leg press into the diving board, increases momentum.

On the takeoff, the arm upswing must be done in combination with an ankle-and-leg snap. The ankle snap provides the same type of power that lets a baseball player slug the ball over the centerfield wall, or the golfer hit a long drive.

While all this leg-and-arm motion is going on, your head and neck are locked, motionless, to your body. The head is the point of rotation, the axis around which all dives revolve. The body motion is used in the follow-through.

Your body remains on the diving board until your arms

have completed their lift past the chin, to the point where arms and hands are at the peak of the hurdle.

The perfect arm swing is like outlining one half of a ball. The imaginary circle is in front of you, from the midpoint of your hips to a point above your head between eyes and nose. (This may vary according to the diver's strength and inherent rhythm.) As your arms swing downward, they complete the outline of the ball. But if you swing too far back past your hips, your entire body will lean back. Your head, torso, and spine will not be directly over your feet, and maximum lift will be lost.

Remember that the separate parts of a dive all add up to its ultimate execution. The approach, hurdle, drop into the board, and takeoff are interdependent. If one segment is poor, the other facets suffer. A good example is that the takeoff accounts for 90 percent of a dive. Obviously, this is an important technique to perfect. But the perfect takeoff depends upon a proper approach and hurdle. You can't have one without the other.

Helpful hints—takeoff

• One training technique I recommend is having someone hold in front of you a stick or rope to hurdle over. Gradually increase the height. This is a good way for a diver to begin to develop that explosive high hurdle.

The obstacle forces you to push harder with your pressing, or power, leg, and to thrust more forcefully with your hurdle leg. Make sure your ankle is

Straining to touch the stick with both hands. Eyes remain fixed on the stick.

snapped as hard as possible and your toes are pressed and pointed to clear the obstacle.

● To improve the takeoff (as previously mentioned), reach for a stick held approximately three feet from the end of the diving board. It should be high enough to force you to stretch with both hands while looking at the object to be touched. Have it raised to a height where it will be necessary for you to strain to reach it. Make sure you always land in balance and at the same distance from the end of the diving board on each dive.

It is important that you focus on your hands *and* the stick to be touched. This teaches you not to look at the water as you spring from the board. These exercises build timing, rhythm, and power.

● Practice flattening your feet after they have disappeared completely under water. This produces a rip (no-splash) feetfirst entry.

● On feetfirst jumps, you must "stand up" on your entries to straighten out your entire body. To illustrate this, sit in a chair and stand up; note how you must lift up your chest and straighten your back. Keep your head and neck rigid and pointing straight ahead. This places the entire body weight over your feet.

Compulsory Dives

GROUP I—FORWARD DIVES

FORWARD DIVE STRAIGHT (LAYOUT)

ONCE THE FORWARD takeoff and jump have been mastered, it is time to work on a forward dive straight, commonly known as a swan dive. The diver simply assumes a straight body position, with arms extended perpendicular to the shoulders. It is the most difficult dive to do well consistently.

To get the feeling of the proper body position, lie flat on your stomach on the pool deck, with your arms extended over your ears and head. Now spread your arms, while keeping your head and neck rigid. Your chin will rise slightly off the deck. Simultaneously raise your toes

Working on the pool deck to get the feel of the proper body position for the forward dive straight.

and feet off the ground. Keep the slightest possible arch in your back. Your arms are perpendicular to your shoulders, yet not back of the shoulder-line, with your arms and palms pressing on the ground. Your body position should be that of a flying cross—*not* emulating a sea gull plunging for fish or the outline of a swept-wing jet fighter-plane.

As you lift off the diving board, your arms swing upward; then, just at the peak of flight, your arms should

39

be fully extended perpendicular to the shoulder-line, with your head remaining stationary. As your body rotates over the top of the dive, keep your arms locked into the cross position. Ideally, peripheral vision will pick up your extended fingertips, with your palms facing the water.

Trial-and-error is the only way to gauge how much you should press back with your legs and heels as you leave the diving board, in order to have a controlled rotation for the drop or descent from the peak of your dive.

Do not duck your head at the peak of the orbit or change your arm or head position. Your entire body (chest, torso, hips, thighs, legs, toes, and feet) will follow through in the same position from the peak to the descent. An altered head or arm position will change the body line. Focus your eyes on the point of entry.

A few feet from the water, close your arms directly over your head. Squeeze your biceps and shoulders over your ears. Lock your elbows and clasp your hands firmly, so that the palms will break the water's surface.

As your hands strike the water, make sure they do not split apart, and keep your head in position. If you duck your head by dropping it to your chest, or raise it, you will not make a rip entry, but a big splash!

Upon entry, every muscle in your body is taut, from fingertips to toes. Stretch for the bottom of the pool. Don't allow the force of the water to make any part of you buckle. The ideal entry will see the toes enter the

A perfect entry. The body is straight, with no arch, and maximum stretch. Shoulders are squeezed over the ears. The hands are flat and locked for a "rip" entry.

same "hole" where the hands made their entry.

As far as I am concerned, Greg Louganis has the most perfect forward dive straight. He makes it look effortless. He continually puts together a perfect approach, high hurdle, complete press and arm position, and no head movement, for consistent rip entries. (By the way, I am Greg's coach, so I might be a bit partial to his style.) The only criticism I do make is that Greg sometimes has a tendency to get his arms back a bit from the straight cross position, and this causes his head to drop slightly.

Helpful hints—forward dive straight

• As an aid in learning the forward dive layout, have a stick or crossbar held up and make yourself lift over it. You should have to struggle to clear the bar. This helps you maintain a proper distance from the end of the board.

This exercise also teaches you to go all out at all times. For perfection, you must give a constant 100 percent on every dive. A diver used to exerting a lesser effort won't be able to handle the extra drop and lift on the rare occasion he goes all-out, and that dive could be a disaster.

• Keep in mind that it is almost impossible to hit the diving board so long as you dive with your legs, complete the arm press, follow through, and don't move your head toward the board (especially inward) or the water. Remember the axiom, "The body goeth where the head taketh."

• A forced or hurried takeoff will cause you to

Working on the forward dive straight with the aid of a crossbar. The head-and-arm position is good, but there is too much arch in the back.

go over on your back, because your legs will be pulled behind too rapidly. If you pull back with your chest, your legs won't come up behind, and you will soon know what it feels like when a ninety-meter ski jumper lands on his feet!

• Beginners tend to start setting their position too early. This causes them to "cut" the board, which means the diver leaves the board before it has thrust him up and away. This results in the diver becoming airborne too close to the board.

Always fully extend your legs and follow through on the arm press with no movement of your head (keep a mental picture of jumping over that crossbar). This sets up the perfect orbit for a beautiful forward dive.

• If you do miss a perfect takeoff and don't get into the right flight pattern, never give up! Fight the law of gravity and make the best of the dive. Do not quit and flatten your feet or spread your legs. *Every competitive dive counts!* Giving up on a dive at the Nationals or Olympics could mean the difference between a 0 dive and a 3-pointer. It could make the difference in getting into the finals or getting a gold medal. This has happened at all levels of competition. In 1968, a defending Olympic champion did a forward dive, bent her legs, and missed the finals. Why? She was discouraged after a poor takeoff in a practice dive, and simply gave up. *Always complete a dive.* Half a point is better than no points.

44

• A diver may go past the ninety-degree, or per-pendicular, entry point, when the legs leave the board too firmly. Missed timing or rhythm off the board will cause you to lose control. If you do not press back firmly enough with your heels on takeoff, or if you pull back on your chest, you won't tip over. You will wind up going short. If you do end up short, don't duck your head; lift it back and pull your heels back to tip the dive forward.

If you have doubts, do (or watch) a forward somersault straight (layout) and note that an ex-perienced diver has his or her head up when he or she somersaults forward in the layout position.

• Many divers swing their arms down, around, and then close them in a position *other* than directly over the head. This results in a poor entry and spoils the beauty and effortlessness that should be dis-played on forward dives straight. It also lessens the chance for a 10-point score. Hands swung down and forward mean the diver's hands will be catching the water before they reach directly over his or her head. This could cause you to flip over.

• A most common fault is that during descent the head is dropped in search of the water and/or the entry point. Your head must not move!

• It is most difficult to rip an entry (enter with no splash) if arms, hands, and wrists aren't strong enough to withstand the blow of the water's surface.

Divers must strengthen their wrists. Daily handstands are advisable. The arch of your back must be worked out of the handstand, so that your body lines up straight. Lie on the deck to get the feel of straightness. Have someone work with you to observe that you are doing a no-arch handstand. You can also line yourself up against a wall to get the feel of straightness. Remove footwear to allow yourself to stretch your toes to the maximum (and not leave footprints on the wall).

- Another method to practice lining up your

Practicing the stretch for entry. Right now, there is too much of an arch in the back

when the diver tightens her stomach muscles, the arch disappears.

body for straight entries is to lie on your back with your legs straight out and your arms stretched over your ears with your hands clasped over your head. Tighten your stomach muscles to press the hollow of your back (lumbosacral arch) out and against the floor. Practice this daily. Soon it will become an unconscious effort on your part, every time you reach for the water, to instinctively tighten your abdominal muscles and get the sway-back out of your entry.

47

GROUP II—BACK DIVES

TAKEOFF

It is essential to gain proficiency in the back-dive takeoff, for all back dives (straight, pike, multiple back-flips, etc.) originate from this position.

Begin with the basic forward, but there will be no hurdle from the board. At about six inches from the end of the board, pivot on whichever foot feels more natural. You are now facing the fulcrum and back of the board with your back to the water. Your arms are stretched out forward to shoulder level.

Now step back with either the right or left foot so that all five toes (especially the small toe) and metatarsals (the bones forming the ball of the foot) are on the board. Too many divers (I would guess out of fear) place only three or four toes and the metatarsals on the board. They think this will carry them out further, or lessen the chance of striking the board. Remember that you dive with your legs—they lift your entire body on and away from the board, enabling you to achieve proper orbit. It stands to reason that with less than your whole foot on the board, you cannot implement the maximum amount of push and will have a greater chance of slipping from the board.

Your feet should be positioned with heels together and feet apart. Heels-together lessens the chance of split-knee takeoffs; dives with legs apart are poor dives. Placing your feet apart widens the base for maximum momentum or push into the diving board; it also decreases the possibility of losing your balance and veering laterally (''casting'') to the right or left side.

You will learn to get the rhythm of the board by keeping your body at attention, with arms outstretched at shoulder level. This arm position aids in maintaining balance.

Your eyes are fixed on the far end of the diving board. Your head is level. Your head, neck, spine, hips, and legs are straight.

Pull back on your hips to keep a perpendicular line with the bent diving board. Suck in your stomach and lock your knees. Lower your arms to your sides. You should now be standing at a position of attention.

Slowly raise your arms as you press your feet into the diving board. Raise your heels. The board will now begin to flex. After three or four presses of the board (by raising and lowering the heels slightly), the rhythm of the board should be established.

The more the heels are raised, and the higher the arms are placed, the greater the movement and push into the springboard.

I prefer that my students begin with slow board movement. This makes it easier to gain timing for the eventual hard press, ankle push, and lift. The better the diver's rhythm, the better the lift.

Concentrate by looking at a fixed point at the far end of

Try to copy Greg's back dive body position. With arms extended, and head and eyes fixed, rise on your toes just prior to the downward circular press of the arms.

the diving board. Do not let the distance vary.

If the distance lessens, you are leaning into the diving board by dropping your chest forward or your head down. If the distance increases you are either pulling off the board too early with your head or neck, or simply falling back.

To obtain maximum push on the back lift, your arms should be brought up from their position at the sides of your body until they are reaching straight up above your head. This motion should coincide with the upward rhythm of the board.

Your back remains at a right angle to the board, with your head at the same angle to your back.

All your weight is now into the board. Your head and shoulders are positioned over your feet. Do not purposely overbend your knees on the press. Make a conscious effort to lock your knees. As you begin to raise up, your arms raise and your legs push. Make sure your elbows remain straight. Your eyes follow your hands as they come into view. Your arms continue upward in a circle. Complete the circle by getting your arm swing back to where you started on your downward press.

Make sure your legs remain under your body and that your entire body weight is over your feet as your legs push off against the board.

Spring off the board with elbows locked, no head movement, and no arch in your back. As you lift off, your arms come through in a half circle as they swing firmly downward without pushing past the midpoint of the hip line. Arms swinging too far back cause a body to pull too far back; too far forward robs you of a good ride off the board, and you fall into the diving board. Arms are used for timing and rhythm, to allow the diver to explode off the springboard with the powerful leg-and-ankle snap.

Many beginners put too much arm and back into the takeoff and wind up much too far from the end of the diving board. As they push, they start falling backward and the board thrusts them out too far. The ideal distance at which to land is no more than three feet from the end of the diving board. When your feet hit, you should be able to touch the end of the board simply by reaching out with your hands.

BACK DIVE STRAIGHT

Once you have confidence in your back takeoff jump from the springboard, you are ready for the back dive.

This will be a strange sensation for the novice. Back dives are not be attempted from the pool deck. The dive requires more height than you can get at poolside, and there is a real possibility of diving into the pool wall.

Position yourself standing backward on the diving board (as you have already learned), clasp your hands in front of you, and start reaching backward for the water by following your hands and arms with your eyes. Keep your head well back and arch your back as you fall. You

Extend hands over head, with eyes focused on hands. Arch continuously as you fall back. Keep reaching for the water. There should be no bend in the knees.

will fall into the water headfirst every time, so long as you do not panic and bend your knees. This will cause you to go flat on your back or to scrape your back if your head and arms thrust backward before the board pushes you away from the end. With repetition, you will gain more and more confidence in pushing into the board, springing off harder and harder, and thereby getting higher and higher!

A competition back dive is similar, but you take a definite lift off the board, as in the back jump. As you do your back lift, instead of keeping your legs and feet downward as you push up and back in a jump, you actually follow through with your own lift. As your arms and hands come into view, your eyes, head, and chin follow through. Your chest is thrust upward, and at the peak of the dive, when you feel as though you are about to drop your arms, spread into a cross. Your head goes back to permit your eyes to see the water. Do not *throw* your head back—press it back slowly. Your feet not only push away from the diving board, but come up toward you in the same arch as the dive. Your body must go over that imaginary bar.

Hold the cross position until a few feet before you hit the water. Now, your arms and shoulders close over your head and ears. Clasp your hands, with the thumb of one hand on top of the other hand. The fingers of one hand grasp the fingers of the opposite hand. Then, reaching for the surface, hit and part the water with most of the palm of your hand. Your entire body (toenails to fingernails) stretches to its fullest extent as you head for the bottom of the pool.

Helpful hints—back dive straight

- When a dive seems to be going "long" (over on your stomach), it is usually caused by your arms whipping you off the diving board, or your head snapping back quickly to spot the water (instead of slowly, as your eyes look for the water). Another reason is that as you spring from the board, your feet may be lifting off too strongly, as if you were kicking both feet up. Correct this by keeping your heels down and slightly back as you lift off. Push your chest and entire body upward.

- Going "short" (over on your back) usually results from not pushing hard enough with your legs, not pressing your legs forward enough as you go into orbit, or pushing your heels back too hard as you take off. Remember to implement trial-and-error to get the proper feel.

THE CROSS

After the back dive layout has been mastered, you graduate to using your arms and diving in a "cross," which is similar to the diving position in the forward dive. This position is never set until maximum lift has been reached. Not only does the arm position look beautiful, it gives the diver greater control as well.

55

The head remains rigid, and the back straight, as the eyes watch for toes and hands to touch. The same technique is employed in the reve dive pike.

BACK DIVE PIKE

The lift for this dive is the same as for the back-dive takeoff. The press and lift is also the same, with your eyes on a fixed point near the end of the diving board.

On this dive, as your arms pass in front of you, your head and eyes *do not* follow the hands up. You do push your chest up. At the peak of the lift, with rigid head,

56

neck, and arms stretched over your head and ears, your legs are brought toward the torso.

Your back and shoulders are in a straight line as your legs come up to a 45-degree angle to the water. With no head movement, touch your toes (or ankles) by dropping your hands down to your toes and feet. After the touch, leave your legs at that angle and pivot away from them by lying back to straighten out the body. Look for the water by pressing your head back slowly, with your arms spread into a cross. If you do not wish to spread into a cross, clasp your hands in front of your chest, then stretch for the water and your entry. *Do not throw your arms back, or you will go over!*

This is one of the basic dives that many divers find easy to score consistently well on. This is true because a diver can adjust more readily if the takeoff is not exactly right.

On the back pike, it is possible, with experience, to computerize your body immediately after takeoff. For example: If your takeoff has not lifted you as high as desired, you can compensate by piking a little quicker, or by bringing your legs higher or coming out or pulling away from your legs more firmly with your back, head, and arms. If you know you are going over, you can bring your legs to less than the 45-degree angle, and after the touch, even drop them down slightly.

The advantage of the pike position over the layout is that in the layout, it is difficult to hide any adjustment attempts.

57

GROUP III—REVERSE DIVES

ONE-FOOT TAKEOFF

When I was in competition, the reverse dive was known as a gainer. You might also hear it referred to as a Mohlberg—the name of the German diver who invented the maneuver.

Set the fulcrum all the way up, to stiffen the board. This facilitates kicking up with one leg as you push off with the other leg. (Coach Dick Smith refers to the pushing leg as the power leg, and I shall use this apt description in the text, or as the "pressing leg" on the springboard.)

Now, you may be asking yourself a common question: "How can I possibly do a reverse dive without hitting my hands, or even my head, on the diving board?" Not a bad question, considering the fact that you'll have to make a forward takeoff and then make your head and body go backward *toward* the diving board. Actually, once you get the hang of it, this is an easy process. It also presents little danger. If you have ever kicked a ball or scrap of paper lying on the ground, you have knowledge of the basic physical motion required.

A minimum of four steps are needed. If you are right-handed (and -legged), stand on the front of the board, with your heels at the end. Take four steps, beginning with the leg that will *not* be your kicking leg then turn and face the water. Take easy steps—left-right, left-right, left-right, then left—and kick with the right leg (if you wish to employ a left-leg kick, the first step will be on the right foot).

As long as you remember that the reverse dive is done with *the legs,* you are in no danger of coming into contact with the diving board. A powerful upward kick with your bottom leg straightening on the kick and no head move-

On the next to last step of the one foot takeoff the arms swing back as the takeoff leg steps to the board end. Eyes focus on the end of the board. The head and back remain straight.

59

ment until completion of the leg action, assures a safe flight into the water.

On this dive, your arms come back on the next-to-last step. Your back remains perpendicular to the board as you step into it with your takeoff leg. Your kicking leg continues its motion and follows through as if booting a football.

Do not pull your head back until you can see your feet coming up. Swing your arms (keeping elbows straight)

Kicking up and out on the running reverse dive. Look at the foot of the kicking leg as the power leg does an ankle snap.

Following the kicking leg to the training stick on the running reverse dive. Eyes view the kicking foot. The power leg, kicking in the same direction, comes up to meet it.

up in rhythm with the kick, and push with the power leg. Your arms move upward. Your head and eyes follow your hands up and back.

After you see your foot, your power leg makes its push up, forcing you away from the board as the power leg comes up to meet the takeoff leg. The takeoff leg (right leg for right-handers) can also be called the hurdle leg.

It's a good idea to practice this body action while standing in the water. This allows you to feel how hard the kick must be to permit your leg to rise up to hip level, a necessary position for a successful reverse dive.

Now try the dive from the one-meter springboard. You will soon discover that following the kick, the kicking leg must keep going in an upward direction in order to rotate your torso and chest so that your back faces the water and your face, the diving board. Swing your arms back in reaching for the water. Clasp your hands to make your entry.

Remember, it is your legs that start the rotation of the dive *before* you pull your head and arms up and back. If your head and arms start the rotation before your legs, you can hit the diving board! Most beginners will kick out much too far (the law of self-preservation), and will have difficulty in getting into a headfirst entry position.

TWO-FOOT TAKEOFF

Once you are capable of doing a gainer from a stepped takeoff, the two-foot takeoff is the next dive to be attempted. The technique employed is the same as that used by Olympic-caliber divers for their reverse 2½'s or "running" reverse dives, from atop the ten-meter platform.

Take a stance on the one-meter board with both feet on the end of the board. Your arms swing upward (as in all forward dives) as your feet press into the board for the liftoff. Your legs come off with a strong ankle snap, with a simultaneous motion similar to kicking someone with both feet. Wait for the hands to come into view before tilting your eyes and head backward. At peak height, your back arches. Spot for entry as soon as the water is in view.

Acclimation to the dive from the board will be enhanced by some preparatory work while immersed in the pool. Stand in the shallow end of the pool. The water level should be low enough to allow you to stand comfortably, yet deep enough so you won't hit your head on the jump landing. Do your jump, forcing both legs upward, as in the back flip. The resistance you feel is similar to that encountered in diving from the board. Allow legs and hips to follow through as they do on the board.

This leg action, in combination with no head movement prior to the straightening of the legs and with the arm swing to carry him or her up and out, insures that the diver will not come into contact with the board.

Helpful hints—reverse dive

- A stick or rope is an excellent tool to use when learning this dive. Have a friend hold either of these objects out beyond the board at an appropriate distance. On the one-step approach, it provides you with an excellent target to kick through.

- When working on the two-foot takeoff with a spring, have the stick held approximately three feet from the end of the board. This gives you a concept of the distance that must be reached. It forces you to lift high, while at the same time pushing your legs and pelvis forward and upward.

63

• Reaching your hands upward with no arm bend helps you keep in rhythm with the diving board.

• If you can see both your hands *and* the stick, it is easier to know when to arch over into the imaginary "Fosbury Flop."

• Access to a trampoline and spotting belt will accelerate perfecting this dive.

REVERSE DIVE LAYOUT

This dive is done in the same manner as the back dive, except that it requires a forward approach.

The fundamentals remain the same: the walk, hurdle, lift, follow-through with the arms, and locking of the head and neck.

As you begin to press into and off the diving board, your arms take a hard swing up and out. As your hands come into view, your head and chest follow. Your hands reach up and over to a point above and in front of you. If your arms swing back too quickly, your head will tilt backward too rapidly prior to completion of the lift, and you will run the risk of coming dangerously close to the board.

Reach firmly out and up. As you see sky and hands, it is time to push your chest, hips, and feet upward in the same arc.

Force depends on lift. The harder your upward arm swing, the more powerful the upward motion of your chest. This results in a proper pull of your hips in the same arc of inertia.

Hands reach for the sky, with head up, looking at hands. This takes place just before hands drop to the "T" position. This is the same technique as used in the back dive.

Snap your ankles to lift yourself into the air.

As you near the peak of the dive, your chest remains high as your arms spread from your sides into the cross.

At the dive's peak, arch over that imaginary high-jump bar into a "Fosbury Flop." Your head tilts backwards as your legs and hips lift up. If fundamentals have been properly executed, you should not need to do any snapping, hyperextending of your head, or severe back arching.

Look back, never relaxing your neck. You should see

65

hands, sky, diving board, and water (in that sequence).

As you begin to descend, focus your eyes on the water as your body begins to pull out of the arc. Tighten your hips and stomach. Pull your hips back. (Imagine you are about to be struck in your belly button by a fist. You would pull back with your hips and lock your stomach muscles. It's the same motion.)

As you prepare to enter the water, your arms and shoulders close directly over your ears. Your eyes remain fixed on the entry point.

As contact is made with the water, flatten your hands to absorb the shock. The ideal entry is perpendicular to the water. Your body stretches for the bottom of the pool!

Helpful hints—reverse dive

• How much to press back with your feet or to push them upward to maintain momentum, will depend on the initial acceleration from the lift.

I like to have my divers reach for the sky, or lift with their arms swinging upward at one shoulder-length's length apart. This position makes it harder to pull too fast with one arm. I instruct many beginning divers to touch their hands together as they rise above their shoulders and chin. This insures that both arms will move in tandem, and that they will reach the peak together prior to their separating into the "cross" position.

• I've witnessed too many divers at age group meets, and even at the Nationals, establish position too quickly. This does not permit a diver to reach the maximum peak of the dive, and it results in cutting the dive too close to the board and never gaining real control.

Always finish the lift before starting into the dive. Then reach to get your chest up and spread into the "cross" at the dive's peak. This permits good form in tipping over to complete the maneuver with the accepted appearance for a pretty dive.

After you have reached your orbit, do not pull with your arms unless you feel you are going to be short. If you *know* you are entering short, pull consistently, as if you were going to enter far down at the other end of the pool.

If you feel you are going over, pull out the arch to compensate. This corrective measure will become second nature with time and experience.

• The regular closing motion is simple. Bring your hands together directly over your head and ears. Do not make the common error of swinging your arms back down and around, and *then* closing.

REVERSE DIVE PIKE

Press off the diving board as in the back dive straight. Your body must be perpendicular to the board, with your feet under your body. Reach high with your arms. Do not

67

move your head, or drop or lift your chin, until just before the peak of the dive.

Pike by bringing your feet and legs up to your torso. Back and torso remain straight as your legs are brought up to just beyond a 45-degree angle. Drop your hands to meet and touch your toes. *Look* at your hands touching the toes, then drop back from your legs, keeping them held still. Your arms drop out for rhythm, not power (unless you are in trouble).

Helpful hints—reverse dive pike

- Consider practicing this move in the pool to gain the feeling of pushing your legs upward and to experience the resistance.

- Another good prediving technique is to hang from a crossbar and bring your legs up to you. This aids in developing the straight upper-body position needed in this dive, as well as in the back dive pike. Stomach muscles are strengthened as well.

- Using a trampoline and spotting belt is an ideal way to learn any of these fundamental groups of dives.

REVERSE DIVE TUCK

(These instructions are also applicable to the back dive.)

The tuck is achieved by bringing your legs to your torso with thighs up against your chest. Almost immediately after the tuck, you kick out parallel or at a 45-degree angle, depending upon the amount of momentum obtained as you first unwind (as in the pike position).

This is an excellent dive to work on, for when you pop out of reverse 1½'s or 2½'s, as well as back 2½'s, you will have to kick out to stop the somersault action, and this motion is similar to kicking out of the tuck. You *must* kick out on the above dives. It is the *only* way to stop your centrifugal force.

If you fail to kick out and then compound the error by jerking your head back, the result will be a belly flop. This will be a sight to behold, and a feeling you will long remember!

GROUP IV—INWARD DIVES

In the 1940's, we referred to this dive as the "cutaway dive." The diver cut away from the board in order to execute the dive—going in toward and facing the diving board.

The most common mistake made is to duck your head in hoping to miss the diving board as your body falls away from the plank. In reality, if the lift is not completed with your legs, and your head ducks into the board, your chances of striking the board increase!

When I was learning the inward 2½ (this was in the late 1930's), Dick Smith and I had the same diving coach. Our mentor would encourage us by suggesting that we not fear hitting our faces on the board, for it would only improve our looks! I don't know if it was fortunate or unfortunate for us, but my friend Dick Smith and I never had the topography of our faces altered while diving. That happened as youth faded and wrinkles appeared. So much for my reminiscing . . .

INWARD DIVE TUCK

The inward dive tuck is easier than the inward pike or layout. In order to get over the fear of hitting the board, you must start with a back-dive stance. Initiate arm-and-heel action as described in the back-dive takeoff. Press your arms upward simultaneously as you push with your legs, feet, and ankles to push your hips up and back.

Raise you arms high on the lift and lock your head, neck, and back into one unit as your hips are lifted up and out. Then your arms come down, with elbows fixed, as your hips come up. Pull your knees into a tight tuck. You will be surprised how easy it is to make a headfirst entry.

It is important to note that the quicker your arms come through for the press and the quicker your hips come off the board, you will better your chances of *not* hitting the diving board, providing you do not drop your head and chin down on your chest to look for the water before your legs take you off the springboard. Nor will you have difficulty getting in headfirst, provided that you do not raise your head, causing you to fall backward before your legs push the board when you are trying to dive forward.

70

INWARD DIVE PIKE

Stand backward. Position yourself on the board, as practiced, facing the fulcrum.

Keep your back perpendicular to the board as you press. Your head and hips should be positioned over your feet. Keep your eyes fixed on one spot at the end of the board. During the press, you should not bend your elbows or knees (any bend will be the subconscious flex mentioned earlier).

Press hard with your legs, as your hands swing downward without your arms swinging back past the hip line. Do not allow your chest to drop over or past the perpendicular angle with the board. Keep your neck and head rigid.

Your arms should reach up high as your ankles snap and your legs extend and push up your hips. Your legs should drive your hips up and out, as if they were coming up to meet your hands. Your head remains in a locked position. *Don't drop your chin.*

As your hips rise, bring your arms down to your toes. Keep your back square and your shoulders straight. Your hands touch your toes (or ankles) at the peak of the dive. Your head remains fixed, with eyes set on the point of entry.

Keep this head-and-hand position as your legs press away and lift above your head.

Aim forward slightly as you stretch out for the entry.

Momentum will carry you over if you attempt to splash down at a perfectly perpendicular angle. This also applies to forward and inward somersaults.

Upon entry, your arms are raised over your head, and your biceps and shoulders are squeezed against your ears. Your hands reach for the bottom of the pool.

Helpful hints—inward dive pike

• As in all back lifts, you must complete the straight arm press *and* leg lift on all inward dives, be they pike, straight, 1½, or 3½.

• The crux of the dive is in locking your head and neck and not dropping your chin, or moving your upper torso into the board until your feet have lifted off the diving board.

• Don't move your chest backward trying to get away from the board, because that will put you too far from the end.

• Don't lift your chin as you start the press, as this will force you to fall back by changing your axis of rotation.

INWARD DIVE STRAIGHT

The takeoff is the same as in the inward dive pike. The position assumed for the inward dive straight is the same as for the forward dive straight. Once the position is set, it does not change. The entry is the same as in any headfirst dive.

To gain maximum press on the inward dive straight, head and eyes look forward, arms press upward past shoulder level before the heels lift back.

The big difficulty on the dive is not to push your hips up and out before you finish the follow-through, with the arm lift at least at shoulder level—although I prefer at least as high as your chin and nose, with the usual straight arm press, head and neck locked.

As your arms come into view, push and kick your heels back and upward to catch up with your arm press

73

without bending at the waist. At the same instant you kick your heels up and back, spread your arms into a "cross," or swan, position. Once the "cross" position is set, not a muscle moves until you close for the entry. A perfect inward dive straight will appear as effortless as a forward dive straight.

With head locked and arms on the cross position, the legs come up behind. This position is held until you are ready for entry.

Helpful hints—inward dive straight

- Have a stick held behind you to reinforce the importance of the fundamental takeoff. Be sure to remain on the diving board until the arm lift reaches at least shoulder level. This is a signal to start lifting your heels behind firmly and forcefully.

With the stick held behind you, kick at it vigorously with your heels. If this does not work, then, as you take off, have the stick placed in front of your shins and push your legs behind. This subtle technique should soon get the message across as to the proper leg action.

- The inward dive straight is the same in every way as the forward dive straight, except that you are facing the diving board and must dive into it with perfect timing to get the proper rotation and angle of entry for a 10-point dive.

GROUP V—TWISTING DIVES

FRONT DIVE HALF-TWIST LAYOUT

This is a most complex dive. Even though the body twists, the entry is the same as in a back dive straight.

Since the twisting motion is difficult to master, I think it appropriate we spend some time covering the topic in detail before actually going through the technique of this dive.

The mechanics of a half twist are controversial. The Russians have a technique that appears very jerky and robotlike to the American diving eye, but the method is technically correct. Their divers turn rapidly at the peak of the dive. The primary twist is with the hips and head. Arms remain above shoulder level, and they spread at the peak into a back dive.

The first time I saw this, I gasped, for I was sure the diver had made a mistake. But when I saw that they executed the dive well nine out of ten times, I had to concede. You can't argue with success.

The American method involves a slow roll into the twist, finishing after the peak of the dive. The Russians conclude the twist at, or just prior to, the peak of the lift, or hyperbole. They do a back dive from the peak through the descent. Most of our divers do the half twist beginning at the peak of the dive and finish about three-quarters of the way down.

How does a diver start the twisting action?

I think coach Lyle Draves has the right idea on the half-twist forward. He instructs his divers to twist at the peak of the dive by lifting their arms a shoulder's-length apart above their head. The outstretched arms and hands then cross, and they spread at the peak of the dive as the diver rotates onto his or her back. The eyes are affixed on the point of entry at all times. The diver then grabs and closes his hands to complete the half twist.

To twist to the right using this technique, pass your left hand underneath your outstretched right hand and push to

To do a half-twister, begin as if it were a swan dive, but keep legs to-gether on takeoff just prior to the half-twist action.

the right. Keep your neck, head, torso, hips, and legs tight. Continue pushing forward and toward the right side of the pool. Your body will automatically turn a half twist. (For a left twist, your right hand crosses under your outstretched left and pushes to the left.)

I like to have my divers try another technique for the twist. To twist to the right, begin with a half twist from the swan, or spreadeagle, position. As you twist, make sure that you sight down your left arm. At the same time, pull back with your right arm straight-armed. Your arms should not drop below the shoulder axis. If this happens, you will have a "cast" or kink in your body while in midair and upon entry.

Either method requires that your eyes fix on the point of entry. Do not duck your head in anticipation of entry; it will alter your axis of rotation, or twist.

In this type of twist, you are revolving on the way down. When dropping out of the peak of the dive, you've done a one-quarter twist. Closing your hands for the entry (some three to four feet above the water) will turn you the other one quarter, completing the perfect half twist.

Always keep your head and neck firm. Do not allow your head to get out of line with your torso, hips, and legs as you turn your chin in the direction you wish to twist. Never lean your head to the side of the twist, as this will cause a cast.

Now let's take a look at the conventional method for a front dive half-twist layout. Either Lyle Draves's or my

Sighting down the left arm and pulling back with the right in the direction of the twist. Be sure that the left arm stays above shoulder level (opposite if the twist is to the left).

method for accomplishing the twist can be implemented.

Begin as you would for a regular forward dive. Go into a forceful forward press as you look straight ahead. Be sure to finish the lift with your arms reaching upward. The amount of heel lift depends on your lift off the board (as in the regular forward dive straight).

As you initiate the twisting action, your eyes should spot your entry point in the water. With chest high and legs pressed back, your right arm (for a right-side twist) pulls back, as your left arm remains extended (as in a forward dive straight). Do not permit your left arm to fall lower than shoulder level, or you will cast over and become crooked in midair.

Your head remains straight, eyes on the target, as your arms and hips implement the rotation. Your right arm remains held high as the left maintains its forward angle.

Your legs come up as your right arm pulls you back over into the twist. Your eyes remain on the point of entry. As your body rotates, your head drops back to find the water. Your arms spread into a back-dive position.

This body position is held until just prior to entry, when your arms come together over your head, your palms flatten, and you stretch for the bottom of the pool as you enter the water.

Helpful hints—front dive half-twist layout

- To learn the twist, try floating in the pool with your body fully stretched out. Reach for the wall and keep pushing with your left hand as if to cross

Closing into a back dive.

your arms. As you push with the left, slide along the wall at an even level.

If you keep your body firm, you will feel the half twist and rotate onto your back. By keeping your right arm straight forward, your shoulder, in a reflex action, will pull up and around, into the back-dive position. When completely turned, you can spread into the straight arm-"cross," or swan, position.

When this motion is perfectly timed with the rise of your legs behind (as in the forward dive straight), you will notice that your legs must come up a little stronger behind as you twist. This results from the shift of weight. If your feet and legs are not brought up firmly behind you, you will tend to wind up short on the dive.

At the dive's peak, when you have finished the dive and are in a back-dive position, the control and entry line-up are the same as in a regular back dive.

Optional (Voluntary) Dives

GROUP 1—FORWARD SOMERSAULTS (1-4½ REVOLUTIONS)

THE KEY here is to start out simple and work your way up. If you cannot do a good forward single somersault, you won't be able to execute a forward 4½ flip.

Somersault dives can be done in tuck or pike position. Layout dives are possible but too difficult to dwell on in this volume.

Divers should use the trampoline as a training tool to perfect somersaults. Multiple somersaults are only possible from a perfect takeoff. The trampoline is a great asset in mastering the necessary moves.

Divers should acquire spatial and visual orientation by degrees. Using the trampoline and safety spotting-belt enables one to throw with abandon. A coach to man the belt is all that is needed. Your horizons are unlimited.

With some practice you will soon be seeing and feeling your front 1½, 2, 2½, 3½, and 4½, with the proper orbits and splashdowns. Not only will you feel your position in relation to the water, but your brain will soon become computerized to the various forward flips. You won't have to count the number of somersaults—you will know when to open for those 2½'s and 4½'s.

Coach Dick Kimball is one of the most remarkable divers in the history of the sport. He says he is able to count his somersaults by seeing the water and spotting the board on each flip and twist!

I was never able to do this. That is why I am a firm believer in learning each dive separately (1, 1½, 2, 2½, 3, 3½ somersaults). When I did a triple somersault I always knew where I was, and when the time came, I looked for my entry-point on those forward 3½'s.

I am sure that if I had access to a trampoline, I could have spotted the water and counted the turns. But when I was on the board, I confess I was terrified. I squeezed my eyes shut, took off, waited for the triple ''feeling,'' then peaked out to spot for my entry. My reverse dives were the same. I felt the double-back and reverse, then kicked out and pressed back for my headfirst entry. That's the way I learned to dive in the late 1930's and early 1940's.

GAINING SPACE ORIENTATION

At this point it is important to develop the ability to judge your body position in relation to the board and the

Working on the trampoline. The diver wears a safety belt, which is at-tached to a spotting rig. I am acting as the "spotter."

water. This is known as "space orientation," or "spotting." Many coaches are using a trampoline and safety belt to teach this technique to beginning divers. Since this method did not exist when I was learning to dive, I cannot speak from actual experience, but I have become a firm believer in the use of a trampoline as an advantageous teaching device for spotting your dives.

A diver can computerize his brain to acclimate himself to the spotting skill with little fear. It is difficult to throw your body into "outer space," not knowing where you are going or how you will land. Working on the trampoline, with the knowlege that you are attached to a safety belt and cannot crash, will eliminate much understandable apprehension. The safety belt is held by a diving coach or an experienced diver.

After a certain amount of practice on the trampoline, you will be ready to "fly solo" off the diving board, knowing exactly where you are at all times. This will be especially helpful, and necessary, when doing multiple twists and somersaults.

The trampoline method has some very creditable advocates: Former Olympic Diving Coaches Dick Kimball of Michigan University, Mission Viejois' Ron O'Brien, and Indiana University's Hobie Billingsly.

One requisite for learning the forward somersault is the ability to control one's anticipation. It is most important to complete the press before beginning to get into dive position.

By this time the approach, hurdle, and takeoff se-

quence is firmly engraved in your mind. On to some
somersault dives.

FRONT SOMERSAULT TUCK

The harder you throw and press the diving board, the
faster and stronger the somersault. The approach, hurdle,
and lift provide the power and height, but only in combination with a perfect follow-through on the arm press. At
the point of maximum bend in the board, both arms
should be straight over your head and ears. Your head
must be straight, with your chin off your chest.

The lift should be completed with your arms straight
over your head. Neck, head, and torso are locked as one
unit. Your arms should be ready for the throw into the
somersault as the diving board pushes you upward.

Your arms throw down, and this forces your hips up
and over. Leg extension adds momentum to the force of
rotation. Your heels lift up toward your buttocks. Your
hips cannot come up at the optinum time if you duck your
chin into your chest before your legs lift off the diving
board.

Clasp both hands at a point below your knees and on
your shins, and pull yourself into as tight a ball as possible by closing your thighs against your stomach and
chest. Once momentum for the somersault has begun,
your head can be brought down to your chest.

The kick-out is begun by having your legs shoot up
with a good amount of kick. Do not move your head. Now

straighten your legs and quickly begin to press down.

Look straight out as your legs continue to press to a "standing-up" position.

At the point of entry "stand up," with chest and back erect. Your chin remains up. Your feet will enter the water at a slight angle, as forward momentum will carry your torso up to a straight entry-line.

As your feet disappear, flatten them to push down the splash.

FORWARD 1½ SOMERSAULT TUCK

Hold your arms high to increase the throw into the circle. At the maximum bend of the board they should be at a point above your head and ears.

Make a forceful takeoff with a forward lean.

At the exact moment the springboard begins its upward thrust, your arms begin to swing downward and forward. Your torso comes downward, with head and neck "locked" to your upper body. Extend your legs. This increases the forward-flip momentum by driving your hips into the circle. The combination of forward arm-motion and leg extension will push your hips above your head.

As your hips rise and your knees bend, quickly bring the arms to the shins. *Do not drop your chin.*

Press your heels upward as you "chase" your legs with your hands. When your legs are almost "caught," your chin can press down into your chest. Grasp your shins with both hands and pull into a tight ball. Your

88

Once the somersault is completed, I spot the water by raising my head and looking out before straightening for the completion of the dive.

head remains tucked in.

Depending on how high you are able to finish your flips and the amount of centrifugal force generated, two options are available for the come-out.

Divers who do not achieve a very high drop come out of the somersault, tuck, and stop their momentum by raising their head and looking at the entry spot in the water. Raise your chest and back (to rip the entry) as your arms are raised over your ears and head. So, as you come around, spot the entry point with your eyes. Begin to break your position. Extend your legs back and up. Your arms and hands swing laterally to a position in line with your hands for entry.

Some divers (like Olympic champion Phil Boggs) generate a great amount of velocity on their somersaults. They will kick out into a pike jackknife position to cease rotation. Their legs kick downward at the water, then come out, as in the front dive pike. So, come out of the ball when looking straight down. You may have to pike your feet forward to a greater degree. This depends on your height and the momentum of the somersault. Extend your legs and kick down in front to stop the momentum. Your arms come out (as in the forward pike) from side to side to over your ears and head. Your toes point to the entry target. Your hands stretch through to the target point and the bottom of the pool.

On both come-outs, the entry is on an angle, to counteract momentum. Every muscle tightens as you stretch for the bottom of the pool.

90

To stop forward rotation on a somersault tuck, kick out into a pike position. Eyes focus on the feet. Do not raise the head.

Beginners should practice both types of come-outs in the single somersault tuck and forward 1½ somersault tuck dives.

Helpful hints—forward somersault dives

- Once again, I think you should have someone hold the previously mentioned pole or stick in front of the diving board. This forces you to reach above your head in order to clear the pole with sufficient height to go into the flip. Eventually this motion will be done instinctively.
- The following pointers should aid in providing an easy and speedy somersault:

While standing on the diving board with both arms extended a shoulder's-width apart over your ears, get into rhythm with the board.

Lock your head and look straight out (not at the water).

As the board bends and begins to come up, push hard and straighten your legs. Simultaneously throw your body into a complete circle. Keep your head locked. Your legs drive your hips up over your head as you throw your arms downward. Your eyes then spot your knees as you grab your shins and enter the somersault.

Never pull your knees apart and go into a "split tuck." Trampoline work can perfect your tuck. Competent

Improper technique for beginning a forward somersault. Note the arms bent at the elbows. On the press and throw-down the arms must be straight.

trampolinists do all their flips and twists with no split in either tucks or pikes. The clean body line thus achieved accentuates the poetry-in-motion for gymnasts *and* divers.

I find it impossible to give specific instructions on how far to throw for a forward 2½ or 4½. The takeoff and complete circle throw of your arms determine the velocity of your flip, and greater velocity than that for a single somersault is needed. Also, these dives require greater leg lift, with hips going up and over a forceful arm throw.

You can now begin to see the importance of learning the fundamental dives in tuck, pike, and layout position. A reverse 2½ or back 2½ after the flips have been completed, really comes out to a reverse dive or back dive in tuck or pike position. All dives are interrelated.

GROUP II—BACK SOMERSAULTS

BACK SOMERSAULT TUCK (202-C)

The lift is the same as in a regular back dive.

The press begins with body weight over the board. Straighten your arms and swing them upward with great force.

Push your legs from the board to carry yourself upward. Then begin to straighten your knees as your arms and hands continue their upward thrust.

Keep a straight back. Raise your chest.

The signal to begin the somersault is when, at the dive's peak, your arms have been extended as high as possible without your having to lift your chin or hyperextend your head to keep your hands in sight. As you spot your outstretched hands, your legs and feet quickly jerk up to your chest, and you grasp your shins. At the moment the shins are grasped, your head pulls backward to start the spin. If this takes place too early, you will not be able to get into a tight tuck.

Keep your eyes open to spot hands and sky in front of you. As you somersault over, you will pick up the water, then the diving board.

When the water is sighted, the kick-out begins. Kick out to a straight position of attention. Your momentum will carry you into a vertical entry. Remain at attention, looking straight ahead, as you enter the water.

Maintain this position as your feet stretch for the bottom of the pool. Flatten your feet as they disappear under the water so that you will not crush your toes on the bottom of the pool.

Helpful hints—back somersault tuck

- The ideal exercise to practice the tuck begins with hanging on to a crossbar or horizontal bar. Quickly bring your thighs and legs up to your stomach and chest. Swing your hips up and over the bar. As you rotate, note how tight your neck becomes, and the rigidity of your head.

• If you do not have access to a gym or a horizontal bar, this exercise can be done in the pool. The water resistance against legs and thighs as you tuck, will strengthen your legs. Working in deep water will also provide the feeling of rotating backward, and a sense of how the head must be used to initiate momentum.

• The common fault of all divers is that they tend to hyperextend their head *before* their feet and legs drive off the diving board. This causes your back to arch and results in either hitting the diving board with your head, or being unable to stop momentum, or centrifugal force. This means loss of control on single, double, or back 2½ somersaults.

Remember, don't pull your head back prior to the completion of the leg lift or permit your arms to swing back too far. This transforms the back dive into a "back flip-flop," and I've yet to see this receive a high score from any judge.

GROUP III—REVERSE SOMERSAULTS

Any diver capable of executing a back flip will have little difficulty learning reverse somersaults.

The advantage in the back flip is that the diver's feet remain on the board for the upward and outward push. On the other hand, the forward takeoff provides greater height to the reverse dive, enabling it to be done higher, faster, and with less effort. You will soon be able to feel on tuck and reverse takeoffs the difference in the push.

REVERSE SOMERSAULT TUCK

The secret of a successful reverse lift, as of all forward takeoffs, is to achieve a high hurdle. Forcefully swing your straightened arms *up* and out as your head and neck remain locked.

Your arms come up and out in a full circle. They should be a maximum of a shoulder's-width apart. Your eyes spot your hands as they pass. Your legs and feet drive off the board, pushing your chest upward in the same arc.

When the flip is done in proper rhythm, your arms are still reaching as your legs come up to meet your outstretched hands. Think of your legs as trying to come up to your arms and over your head, which remains stationary.

At the same instant that you touch your legs with your arms, your head pulls back. This begins the somersault action.

As maximum momentum is attained, your arms and hands come down to grasp your legs at a point just below the knee (midpoint between the ankle and the knee). This is the one time bending your arms is permissible.

As you spot the water for entry, come out of the tuck and begin to go into a standing position. Your arms should be at your sides as you look ahead for entry.

Enter the water at a position of attention. Look straight ahead. Your toes point for the bottom of the pool; carefully flatten them as you break the water's surface.

REVERSE SOMERSAULT PIKE

The same technique applies as in the reverse somersault. The only difference is getting into the pike position, which is done as maximum momentum is reached in the flip.

Your hands come down to grasp your legs just above the calves. Pull your legs in tight as your head pulls in the same direction.

Helpful hints—reverse somersault dives

• Have someone hold a pole about three feet away, and high above the end of the board. Use this as a target to reach for. The pole provides a specific reference point to arrive at before going for the reverse somersault. This exercise assures developing the habit of carrying yourself a safe distance from the board. This exercise can also be practiced on the trampoline: Take a few steps, hurdle, and somersault up and out, landing a few feet from the takeoff point.

• Never lean back into the board on your hurdle. Divers tend to lean backward in the hope that this will enable them to get the reverse done more easily. This habit assures that you will hit the board at some time during your diving career. (At the 1968 Olympics, Micki King broke her arm in this fashion.)

Leaning back on a reverse dive to facilitate the somersault also doesn't allow you to ride the board to its fullest. This forces you to leave with knees bent, another factor that will pull you into the diving board. Watch divers such as silver medalist Jeanne Collier (now Mrs. Kenny Sitzberger) and Keala O'Sullivan. You will see that they never bend their legs on their takeoffs.

• Do not allow your arms to swing so far back that you leave the diving board with an arched back. Leaving the diving surface with an arched back, or bent knees, increases the risk of hitting the board.

• Don't let your head begin the flip before your arms are in position. Keep in mind that it's the upward and outward arm swing with full follow-through, in combination with the leg drive, that gets you away from the board and in position to begin the roll.

• Swinging out of the dive by using your arms like a whip means you stand a real chance of striking the board with your hands or arms. You must *kick out* (review the kick-outs in the back 1½'s and 2½'s tuck) and press back with your head as you look for the water, as your arms press out laterally.

• The ideal distance to travel is no more than three feet from the end of the diving board. This optimum distance is variable, because some divers are taller than others; this factor, combined with the added height achieved from the Maxiflex diving board, could alter the distance anywhere from one to one and a half feet, depending on the dive and the altitude of the diver. The diver may still be doing a hyperbole figure.

If you perform the dive with sufficient height, you should complete your somersaults and be stretching for the water while still well above the diving board.

GROUP IV—INWARD SOMERSAULTS

INWARD SOMERSAULT TUCK

The same lift is employed as in the inward dive pike. The technique changes only at the peak of the dive. At the peak of your lift your arms come down as your hips rise. Be sure to complete the circle with no bend in your arms as they follow through. Flexing your arms too soon will cause a loss of needed power. Press your feet further into the board by a quick flexing action. Stretch your feet and toes as you snap your ankles. Once momentum, or flip, is established, your chin can be dropped to your chest.

Your head, hands and torso "chase" your knees until

you grasp your shins and your body is pulled into as tight a ball as possible.

As your somersault reaches a "sitting" position, it is time to come out of the ball. As your legs thrust straight down, keep your hands remaining at your sides. There is no danger of hitting the diving board so long as your legs are fully extended before you start the downward thrust with your arms and torso. Your chin must not drop to your chest before your feet leave the board.

Look straight ahead as you enter the water, standing at a position of attention.

Helpful hints—inward somersault tuck

- Consistent practice will help you find your personal point of maximum rotation. Repetition will give you confidence in the inward dive. Soon you will be lifting off harder with legs, and will be more aggressive in the downward throw for the somersault.

- The moment of lifting off the board without bending or falling back with your hips before the maximum arm press and lift determines the height and drop of the inward somersault.

- Keep in mind that as you throw for the somersault, your arms swing in a complete circle, spreading no farther than a shoulder's-length. The higher your arms lift, the greater the arm throw.

- The faster you get your arms over your head

and ears (with your head remaining locked), the easier it is for your legs to drive up and your hips to follow during the forward throw for the flip.

• When tucking, be sure not to "split tuck"— that is, move your knees and feet apart. Many divers believe this enables them to spin more rapidly. I won't buy that! The rulebook states that the split tuck receives a one-to-two-point scoring reduction. More important, I find a split tuck aesthetically displeasing and the mark of faulty technique. After all, the name of our sport is "fancy diving."

• This dive, like the forward dives, is simple, for there is no "blind spot." You can see the water even before you are ready for entry.

• There is no difference in takeoff between an inward 1½ tuck or pike. The inward 1½ pike or inward 2½ requires greater power and throw for the greater clearance needed to get your feet away from the diving board.

• The come-out, or preparation for entry, hinges on whether you will have enough time for a pike-out check or a kick-back check, and for lifting your head. Review the forward 1½ and 2½ come-outs. They are virtually the same as the forward 1½ somersault dive.

• If perfectly timed (with arms in position for a maximum throw as the diving board gives you its maximum thrust), the inward 1½ or 2½ could be your best dive, because a perfect takeoff is a most

important element in the dive and provides a great
opportunity to do the dive consistently well.

• When I was competing in the 1952 Olympics, I
felt that the late Skippy Browning had the most
perfect inward 2½ takeoff. In the 1970's, my vote
goes to Mike Finneran. If you ever have the opportunity to see slow-motion films of Mike's inward
takeoffs, you will quickly notice how all the material that has been explained in words *should* be
translated into action when working on the diving
board.

GROUP V—TWISTING SOMERSAULTS

These dives carry a high degree of difficulty, but they
can be the easiest and most consistently well-done group
of dives. Even if a diver over- or under-twists, he or she
can usually make a headfirst entry. Mistakes made in the
takeoff stage can be compensated for in midair with great
ease, in contrast to correcting a forward 3½ or back 2½.

As you watch divers work, note that many of them will
execute beautiful double-twisting forward 1½'s or even
triple twisters, yet miss the simpler forwards or backs, if
the takeoff is less than perfect.

To learn the forward somersault with a full twist, do a
controlled forward dive pike over, then lift your head out
of the pike by pulling it up while pulling your legs behind
you. Kicking your feet and heels back will put you into

an arching layout position.

Bring your chest forward by allowing your seat to drop as you bring your straight legs up to your body. You are actually doing a "seat drop." The re-pike is necessary to control the flip. This will give you the feeling of a forward somersault pike, arching out to a flying forward somersault, then checking into a pike position.

As you progress, you will be required to make one, two, three, or even four twists while in that flying forward position. After the multiple twists, you will have to pike to check the rotation of the twists *and* forward somersault. This is when diving becomes a real challenge.

There are two systems that a diver can employ to do a twisting somersault. Beginners should try both methods to find which is more suitable for personal implementation.

In the first system, you drive your hips up and over as your arms spread into a "cross." The twist begins as soon as your toes have cleared the board.

For a right twist, your right arm bends behind your head, which looks up, turning and spotting your right arm (elbow). Your right hand keeps pulling your right elbow behind your head as it continues turning in the direction of the pull.

At the moment the twist is begun, kick your heels back up; straighten your body so you have a straight body-line (from head to toes) while twisting. You are actually doing a front somersault pike with a layout finish.

Your left arm swings across your chest in the direction

of the twist and hugs the chest wall, with your left hand at a point no lower than just under your right armpit. (Note: If you naturally twist to the left, your left arm goes behind your head and your right arm comes across your chest.) Throw with both arms at the same moment.

As long as your head and chin stay up, and you keep pulling with your arm, you will continue to twist.

To stop the twist, drop your head and chin down and cease pulling in a tight circle. Open the circle into a cross, spread with your arms, and pike out of the layout position. This checks the twist and somersault as you level your head, look at your feet, and prepare to enter the water.

In the second method, the diver twists in the direction of the lead arm.

For a right twist, start the somersault lift with your arms positioned as in the forward somersault pike: above your head and no farther apart than the width of your shoulders.

As your feet and toes catapult from the board, they drive your hips up and over. Simultaneously, you arch out and throw your right arm down and around the back of your head. Turn your head in the direction of your right arm as it pulls and bends behind your head.

The left-arm motion is the same as in the first technique: It comes across your chest toward your right armpit.

As long as your chin and head remain up and pull and turn in the direction of the twist, and the arm pull continues, you will continue to twist. Once your chin is dropped and your arms spreadeagle into a "cross," the twist will stop.

BACK AND REVERSE TWISTERS

The ability to do perfect back and reverse somersaults in a layout position is a prerequisite for twisters. Work on these dives will quickly point out the strengths or weaknesses in your execution of somersault layouts. The secret to this dive is to attain a powerful lift with arms raised and chest high.

For the twist, launch your feet up off the diving board as if you were going to boot a football with both feet. As your feet leave the board, the somersault begins.

If you wish to twist to the right, your right arm swings down in a circle toward your feet. (This motion is actually in counter-action to the flip; it was verified by slow-motion films of divers in action.) Your arm winds down and around to the back of your head. Your head and eyes follow your right hand up and around. You should see both the hand and the sky.

Your left arm simultaneously swings across your chest, and your hand rests under your right armpit. Your head continues to pull in the direction of the twist.

Tighten your buttocks and legs during the twist action.

All through the twist, your feet and legs are coming up in the direction of the somersault. This action provides the continuous power and momentum for the somersault, whether reverse or back twisting.

As in all twists, the twist-and-somersault ceases whenever your chin drops and your arms pull away from your body into a "cross" position.

To pike out of a twist dive, go into a "seat drop." Jump up and bring your legs, with knees locked and feet and toes pointed, right under you, as if you were going to fall on the seat of your pants. Your back is straight and your arms are in the "cross" position. Your chin is down, as you look at your legs and toes. At the same moment, you will see the water. With experience, you will be able to judge how quickly you must come out of the pike dive to enter the water perpendicularly.

You will soon realize that this come-out is no more complicated than coming out of a forward 1½ somersault (with one to four twists in between).

Platform Diving Techniques

PLATFORM DIVING requires jumping with abandon. Once a diver conquers any initial fear of height, he or she is almost sure to find leaping from the tower more fun than working from the springboard. Also, tower dives are easier.

By the time you're ready to begin learning platform dives, you will have had a full introduction to and some experience with the various dives executed from this surface. The springboard dives already perfected will be repeated from the tower. The only additions are the armstand dives. Even these will come easier if you have used armstands or headstands in your training routine. The armstand is necessary for basic entry line-ups and for strengthening arms and wrists to absorb the impact when hitting the water. You will be thankful for those strong wrists when you make an entry from the ten-meter platform.

It is advisable to begin platform diving from a one-meter tower. This is the best place to learn to implement the leg-and-ankle spring and the quick lift with the arm press.

To get used to learning from the platform, practice jumping up and down while reaching, with both arms, as high as possible. Note how much higher you can jump when your arm lift and leg jump are timed perfectly. Now stand on the lowest tower available and do forward and back jumps, entering the water feetfirst, with good body control. Entry to the water should be straight, with your body fully stretched.

STANDING TAKEOFF

Stand on the end of the tower with your feet and toes on the end of the platform. Spread your arms into a "V" position over your head and ears. Swing them down and then up as you jump forward, clearing the end of the tower by three to four feet.

Reaching for a pole or other object held high over your head is useful in learning the proper trajectory needed to clear the tower.

The arm position for platform dives differs from that used on the springboard. On the springboard, you begin with arms at your sides. They then lift upward and swing down for the press and spring. When working on the

The takeoff position for forward or reverse platform dives. Stand at a position of attention, looking straight ahead. Arms are extended into a "Y."

tower, your arms may be in a "cross" position, or held high above your head and ears in a "V" position. Some divers begin with both arms out at a 45-degree angle to the body. The position used depends on the diver's inherent quickness and his or her ability to come through with a rapid arm lift and leg drive to execute a perfect high leap with full body control.

Never hold back on your throw into any dive. To compensate for the loss of spring from the board, it is necessary to throw harder and to jump faster and quicker on tower takeoffs, in order to get into the dive at the proper moment. The jump is the same as off the springboard, without the benefit of the spring. Height depends on your ability, not the propulsion power of the diving board. You are on your own.

Do not sacrifice body position for height. That is, don't drop your chest forward, bend at the waist, and jump, as if doing a standing long-jump. You are not trying to go *out* so much as *up*.

During the jump, your head and chin should be kept in a position of attention. As you jump forward, do not drop your chin onto your chest and push your neck forward to look for the water; this will cause you to land on your stomach more often than on your feet. Look straight ahead on the jump. Spot the landing point with your eyes as your head and chin remain fixed in a position of attention.

Backward jumps are the same, except you dare not drop your chest forward as you jump, or you will come

111

too close to the tower. Do not fall back before jumping, by using your back instead of your legs to jump. This will cause you to go too far out. Ideally on the back jump, you should actually bring your hands forward after reaching high, and touch the end of the tower with your outstretched fingertips as you pass it.

Even after you have become a proficient high-platform diver, you will find regular visits to the one- and five-meter towers beneficial. Additional practice of forward and backward takeoffs will increase confidence and coordination. It also aids in improving rhythm for the powerful explosion off the tower needed to perform the most difficult dives.

GROUP I—FORWARD DIVES

FORWARD DIVE PIKE

Begin with your feet at the end of the platform, and with your toes just at, or slightly over, the edge of the board. Your arms are high above your head and ears, no wider apart than your shoulders' width. Lock your head in position.

Once you can coordinate the downward arm-throw with the upward push of your hips by the leg-and-ankle snap, you will find the front dive pike (or tuck) simpler from this surface than from the springboard.

The amount of downward arm swing depends on the height of the platform. Diving from the one-meter tower requires a more forceful swing (with no head movement) than from the ten-meter tower. If you throw downward too hard from the ten-meter, you will pike too soon and somersault. You'll be ready for the water one meter from the end of the platform, and that leaves nine meters in which you must fight inertia to prevent going over and entering on your back.

Once you have launched into orbit, the dive technique and timing of the dive is the same as from the springboard. The only difference is that the amount of ascent provided by the springboard is not there.

FORWARD DIVE STRAIGHT

To do this dive well, you will have to be able to jump up and out and press back with full control of your legs.

Don't be surprised if, on your first attempt, you jump and wind up in a pike or tuck. This happens when the diver is not accustomed to losing the push of the springboard that gets the legs moving behind the body.

I prefer to teach my divers to do the forward dive straight by swinging their arms down and up, as in a regular springboard lift, then locking them into a swan-dive position as the legs are forced up behind. I see the dive more as a lift-and-dive (although I find no fault with divers who choose to do the dive standing with hands over head, as one does in the forward dive pike).

As you fall out slightly from the tower, jump and spread into a "T," or "cross," position. Lock your head and neck. If you drop your chin and head as you jump forward, you will not be able to keep straight and will bend at the waist on takeoff. This will make it impossible to get your legs moving behind you, and it adds to the possibility of hitting the platform.

According to the height needed, whether from a one- or five-meter tower, you must vary the force of the quick downward arm-thrust by a few inches and get into the "T" with legs and feet pressed behind you, in order to have a controlled dive. The arms extended over the head in this takeoff is the same as in the standing forward dive pike.

FORWARD DIVE APPROACH—RUNNING

You must take at least three steps before your takeoff. I prefer four or more. This running approach initiates momentum and provides enough time to lift your arms straight above your head and ears. As you bounce on the balls of your feet, you should be at a position of attention, with your arms extended up over your head and ears.

There are two ways to raise the arms: They can be brought to your sides and then over your head; or they can be swung up forward, crossed in front of you, then raised over your head, as if you were going into a forward press on the springboard.

The primary difference between the forward approaches on the springboard and the tower is the length of the takeoff, which is longer on the platform.

There is no hurdle on the tower. This is replaced by a low skimming of your feet as your arms are lifted for the eventual snap-off and jump from the platform—as one might do when tumbling. Since you "skim off" what would be the hurdle step, the forward takeoff from the hurdle point is about 1½–2 times longer than on the springboard. You jump low, not high, on the hurdle for takeoff.

Watching gymnastics events is a good reference source for the diver. Watch the leg action of gymnasts. As they wind up for moves in the free-exercise routine, they do quick lifts and jumps, with all the power supplied by their legs. You won't see a tumbler do a high hurdle into a flip—he *skims* along the mat.

Remember, *everything* is quicker on the tower when it comes to forward, backward, or inward takeoffs. Your arms are already in position, so your legs and torso must react faster to get into specific dives.

The instant the dive is begun, your body position becomes the same as on the springboard. Since you are jumping into orbit on your own power rather than using the spring of the board, gaining momentum to start the dive will probably be your major problem.

FORWARD SOMERSAULTS

To be able to throw in a circle, you must assume a body position with arms straight up, perpendicular to the platform. As you hit the end of the runway, your arms

With arms raised, this diver prepares to "skim off" the platform. The knee of the hurdle leg is not raised . . .

As it would be in a similar dive from the springboard.

should be stretched above your head at a point behind your ears. Your head is in a position of attention. As the throw takes place, your legs drive your hips in the same direction as your arms. Your head and torso move downward (as if doing a hard bow) during the straight arm-throw. Grab your shins (if going into a tuck), or keep your legs straight and take hold just under and behind the knees (for the pike).

Review the springboard throw for forward-flip take-offs. The same technique is used on the tower.

The kick-out from the platform flip differs slightly from the springboard version. As you kick out, press back into the entry more slowly. The reason for this is that you are now higher in the air than you were on the board.

The higher you finish your dive, the more time you have to prepare for line-up and entry. The name of the game is to spin and twist as hard and as fast as you can, to have the highest finish of any of the competitors. Diving vernacular terms this procedure, "drop on your dive."

You must be prepared for the entry. The fall from the ten-meter board, if not done properly, can be a painful experience. Entering "short" (on your stomach) or "long" (on your back) can cause much physical discomfort. (Ever hear football players talk of being "blind-sided" by a charging linebacker? Make it *three* linebackers and you can imagine the feeling of hitting the water from the ten-meter tower.) Entry must be at a perpen-

Preparing to throw into a forward somersault. Arms are locked straight over the head, ready to tumble forward. On the takeoff, you first land on the balls of the feet, then the heels.

dicular angle to the water. Your body is fully stretched, with hands and elbows locked and arms and shoulders squeezed over your ears.

You must master the forward 1½ and 2½ from the five-meter tower before going for bigger dives (such as the forward 3½). When I was diving, I did a forward triple somersault from the five-meter platform and worked up to a forward 3½ tuck from the seven-meter tower. This is the type of graduated progression that will help to enhance your proficiency and to give you a higher drop out of your dives.

GROUP II—BACK DIVES

BACK DIVE PIKE

All reverse and back dives are done with a jump from the tower. As you leap, your legs must remain under your torso until your chest has been pushed up. Don't pull off with your back and allow your legs to rise too early. The procedure is exactly the same as in diving from the springboard, except that you are in position much faster.

Just prior to the peak of the jump, your arms should be fully extended over your ears. Your head is straight and your eyes are looking at the tower, which is eight to ten feet away from your takeoff point. If you look down near your feet, your head will drop and you will not be in a straight position on the jump. If your head drifts back before the jump, you will go out too far and go over on your belly.

Bring your feet up to your hands as the latter come down to touch your toes. (Note that you will find it more difficult to bring up your legs on the jump from a stationary tower.) Look at your toes to be sure you have touched and are in the proper position. Do not push them forward as you touch.

Keep a straight line with your head, neck, and back. Then, just as from the springboard, drop away from your legs.

BACK DIVE STRAIGHT

Begin in the standard back-dive position: arms straight with shoulders in a cross position. Your head and eyes focus ahead.

Jump as high and as hard as you can. Reach up in front of you, pushing the chest upward. Your eyes follow your hands as the swing upward to the peak of your jump. At the same instant, your arms spread into the "T." Your head and eyes gently press back looking at the sky, then water, to rotate for the headfirst entry. The amount the heels come back depends upon the jump. Practice and trial and error will set the correct amount of press back with the heels on the takeoff. If the heels come forward you will have a racing dive entry. If the head quickly snaps back while looking for the water, the same belly

The back takeoff position.

flop will result.

After you peak, press into a "T" or "cross" spread, just as in a springboard dive. Keep your arms parallel to your shoulders. If you find yourself stuck on the dive (entering short), press back with your arms to correct the situation.

Never allow your arms to pull back to the point where they crease your shoulder blades and create a concave back position. This is caused by a strained press and too-rapid arm action.

While in the "T" spread, wait for a view of the water. If you snap your head back, you will go over on the dive. Stretch for the bottom as you enter in a handstand-like position.

Helpful hints

- Practice jumping into the water from a one-meter tower or from the pool deck. You will be surprised how difficult it is for the average person to jump uninhibitedly. You can jump and pike, or jump and tuck, and land feetfirst. This is an excellent preparatory exercise.

BACK OPTIONAL DIVES

The idea of graduated progression also applies to the back optional dives. Start out with a back somersault from the pool deck or the one-meter tower. Then go to the back 1½ tuck from the five-meter platform. As soon

On this back double somersault, the arms are too wide apart and too far back. The back, instead of the legs, is being used for momentum.

as you begin work on the five-meter platform, you will note the difference in feeling and momentum from your flips from the springboard, which lifts and throws you into a flip by its whipping action.

Back doubles must be practiced from the five-meter tower until you know where you are at all times. When you see the water, then the pool deck, it is time to kick out and stand up for entry. When you can do this, take the dive to a higher tower. Have someone watch (preferably a coach or experienced diver). As they call out by a "Now" or "Ho," or whistle a signal, kick out of the dive, with your legs straight, into a "seat drop" position for a back 1½, 2½, etc. Then press back, as on a back dive tuck.

When progressing from back doubles (pike or tuck), to a back 2½, don't hold back. Always go for any dive with every ounce of energy in you.

GROUP III—REVERSE DIVES

STANDING REVERSE DIVE (FIVE-METER PLATFORM)

Review the springboard technique for this dive. Bear in mind that you will have to move quicker and with more tumbling strength to get into the proper position, since you will not have benefit of the springboard to propel you into orbit.

125

Looking at the tower to spot for entry on the second flip of a back double somersault.

Once you have learned to jump by swinging both arms from the starting point of either a "V" or a "cross" position (whichever is best suited to your quickness and ability and allows your legs to be used for a maximum jump), you are ready for the standing reverse dive from the five-meter platform.

As you jump, your arms follow through into an arc as your legs jump. Your head is fixed until your hands pass up in front of you, then your eyes and head follow your hands up and back.

Your legs kick up and out, pushing your hips through into the same arc—just as the springboard did for you on your first reverse dive. Remember, *do not* snap your head and back to get momentum for the reverse dive *before* your legs push your hips up and out—or you may wind up kissing the platform with your head.

RUNNING REVERSE SOMERSAULT (ONE-METER PLATFORM)

A standing reverse somersault is the same as a standing reverse dive—you just throw harder. Instead of keeping your legs under you as your hips push upward, your knees now jerk up to your outstretched arms and hands, and your head comes back as you grasp your shins at a point just below the knees in order to get into a tight tuck. You will soon get the knack of the proper timing and will be pleased by the amount of your momentum.

Do not lose sight of the fact that the "running" approach is actually a slow, deliberate walk (review the first running reverse dive from the springboard).

Take four steps, keeping your back perpendicular to

The standing reverse somersault. Momentum for this dive is initiated with the legs. Knees come up to the hands, arms should be straight. On this particular dive, the head is too far back.

the tower; the last step is on the end of the tower, as you kick an imaginary football. Your toes are pointed. The kicking leg follows through, and the power leg must also straighten out in order to catapult your entire body into the air. Simultaneously, swing your arms up and over as hard as you can into the same pattern.

Your head is locked into position. When you can see your kicking foot coming up, then you know you are in the proper position for both arms and hands to be swinging at the same time and reaching high with the knee of the kicking leg and power leg to be grasped up to the chest into a tight tuck to begin your rotation.

Your head snaps back to add to the momentum only *after* your knees are firmly grasped and you make your body as small as possible. This increases your rotating velocity.

Helpful hints—running reverse somersaults

• To do a perfect reverse 2½ somersault, you should be able to make a reverse somersault while working on a tumbling mat. You will soon learn how much to kick and what kind of timing with arm throw and head you need to get you around on the flip.

While working on the mat, practice the difference between a standing reverse somersault and a back somersault. This gives a good idea of the difference between the push-off for the back flip and the reverse flip.

During any mat work, *always* have someone spot for you.

GROUP IV—INWARD DIVES

INWARD DIVE PIKE

This dive is far easier to accomplish off the platform than off the springboard. This is because of the fact that upon takeoff from the platform, the diver already has his or her arms in position for the dive. From the springboard, the diver must do the press, then lift, then get the arms above his or her head and ears before beginning the actual dive.

Stand with your arms above your head—raise them laterally and press them above your head and ears. Lock your head in a position of attention. Start pushing your hips upward and backward.

A quick ankle snap brings your hips up and away from the platform's edge. Your legs and feet are brought up to your outstretched hands.

When doing this dive from the ten-meter tower, your hips must be up, with very little throw-down. A downward thrust of your arms at the improper moment will start the somersault too soon, or cause you to sit back and eventually go over on your back, or land short. Your arms should press downward for only one-fourth of a throw.

Arms must be completely straightened over the head, with the head fixed straight ahead, prior to the ankle snap in the inward dive pike. The ankle snap is followed by the forward and downward throw of the arms.

INWARD SOMERSAULT

Raise your arms above your head and ears. All your metatarsals should be on the end of the diving platform. Your head should be locked, with your eyes focused on a point far enough away so that your chin doesn't drop to see the platform.

Extend your arms, stretching for the sky. You must perform an ankle snap and jump with your legs before your arms pass your ears on the throw for the somersault.

As your arms hyperextend past your ears, it is time to start the throw forward for the inward somersault. Throw in a complete circle toward the tower. The somersault starts as your hips are pushed upward and outward by your legs. The flip is timed with the downward throw of your straight, locked arms. There must be no bend in your elbows.

This somersault must be learned from a half- to one-meter platform, to acquire quickness on the jump and a powerful throw to complete one flip and land on your feet.

GROUP IV—TWISTING DIVES

Review the fundamentals of twisting dives from the springboard. For the most part, they are done in the same manner on the tower. Only now, you don't just press

A perfect takeoff into an inward 1½ somersault open pike. Note the straight arms and locked position of the head.

down, as on the springboard, you tumble off the tower.

The takeoff differs because you must attain proper orbit without the benefit of the spring off the diving board. On forward twisting somersault dives, this disadvantage is compensated for by the fact that your arms are already in position for the throw into the twist when your hips pop up into the pike position.

You will have to throw as hard on a forward 1½ with a triple twist as you would on a forward 3½ pike. The only difference will be that as your hips drive up, your legs will come behind you, thus straightening your body into an arch at the same moment you twist.

As in the springboard twists, going into the layout position provides the momentum for the twist. The initial momentum for a flip is required in order to make the triple or quadruple twister and still have enough time to *pike* for the entry with plenty of drop remaining to complete the dive.

Back twisters are done in the same manner as on the springboard, depending upon which type of throw is chosen to start the twist. A good back-flip-straight position is a necessity.

Remember, on twisting platform-dives, everything is done faster and quicker than on the springboard. The basic lift is the same. Your technique doesn't change, but your takeoff does.

The ability to successfully repeat all these dives (the simple as well as the difficult) depends mainly upon the takeoff. This propels you into a correct orbit so that you

The head is straight with the arms outstretched upon takeoffs into twisting somersaults.

As your arms start the twisting action, your body straightens out for the pirouette.

A proper armstand should be done with no arch in the back. The head is never hyperextended.

can twist or spin with the proper speed and momentum to provide a high drop on the dive.

GROUP VI—ARMSTAND DIVES

Master your ability to do floor armstands to the point where you can achieve the position without wavering. Practice pressing up, as gymnasts do. There should be no arch in your back when in an armstand.

For an armstand fall-over, start the fall by arching your

heels over and past your hands and shoulders. Drop your chin to your chest; this shifts your body weight.

The proper moment of hip-and-elbow bend prior to the arm push-off depends on whether the armstand is being done for a dive into a headfirst or feetfirst landing. "Kip" is similar to the action of a front handspring on the tumbling mat. As your hands strike the mat, your elbows bend, you spring off your hands with your legs going in the same direction, and you move from a pike to a layout position.

On a reverse dive, or armstand cut-through, take a straight armstand. Start falling by arching slightly. Your hands and heels initiate momentum for the fall by arching over.

Now flange your shoulders forward to line up even more with the legs. ("Flange" is the pushing action that takes place when you move your shoulders past the point where your hands are stationary on the tower.) This brings your shoulders and legs over the water. At that instant, you cut through with a flick of your wrist and pull with your arms, bringing your legs down and through.

The armstand with feetfirst cut-through and the kick-out are dictated by the amount of wrist-and-arm push. If the push is strong, you grasp your shins into a tuck position, then kick straight back, at approximately a 45-degree angle to the water, and spread your arms into a "cross." Your head must be kept straight. Now raise your chest and "stand up." Hold your head and neck in a

To begin the armstand fall-over, drop your chin and arch slightly . . .

Legs continue to fall over. Arms remain locked, with hands on diving surface.

Prior to the cut-through, straightened arms push the shoulders past the hands and the body away from the diving surface ("flange"). At that precise moment, the wrists snap and the legs tuck.

straight line with your back. Pull your feet into a position perpendicular to the water by "standing up" continuously.

Just before you strike the water, close your arms to your sides. Enter in a position of attention. As your entire ankle disappears into the water, flatten your feet. This is the way to really rip a feetfirst entry.

To do a reverse dive, grab your knees as you cut through and pull them around to the reverse dive tuck, then kick out (this is explained in the reverse dive tuck from the springboard).

To do somersaults, such as an armstand cut-through reverse 1½ somersault, you must get increased momentum on the cut-through by using your arms to a greater degree and pulling through with your arms and head. Pull on your shins, in the same direction as the flip. This will produce a tight tuck and increase rotation. The come-out is the same as in springboard 1½ somersault dives.

Armstand cut-throughs or armstand fall-overs for forward somersault dives can be practiced from the pool deck. This will help you gain the rhythm and timing necessary to cut through hard enough to achieve the required amount of rotation.

Glossary

A.A.U. The Amateur Athletic Union. An association that sanctions and organizes numerous diving competitions.

Angular velocity. The momentum or speed of the revolutions or twists on a dive.

Ankle snap. Sudden and quick hyperextension of the ankle used to provide power and height to the jump into a dive.

Approach. The initial segment of a dive. This is preparatory to the takeoff and the actual movements of any specific dive.

Arm press. (1) For the armstand dive: kicking up into position using straight arms with elbows locked, or bent arms slowly straightening as legs are gradually pushed up into the armstand. (2) On all forward or backward springboard takeoffs: the action of literally pressing the board downward with locked arms at the same time as the legs and feet press or push into the board to make it flex more.

Armstand cut-through. On an armstand dive, instead of falling forward following the armstand and travelling headfirst, the diver pushes forward to bring his or her feet through for a feetfirst entry.

Armstand dives. Dives initiated from a handstand take-off.

Back dive layout. A backward dive in which the body position remains straight.

Back dive pike. A backward dive in which the diver bends at the waist and grasps his legs, which remain straight, at a point below the knees. He then returns to a straight position for the entry.

Back jump. Jumping backward into the pool from a position facing the diving board or platform.

Back takeoff. Leaving the diving board from a body position facing the board, and rotating away from the board.

Backward dives. Any dive begun from a standing position on the board, with body rotation away from the board to the water. The basic back dives are done in layout, pike, and tuck positions.

Belly flop. An improper form of landing, where the diver makes contact with the water with chest, stomach, and feet at the same time.

Blind spot. The point in a dive when the diver can see

neither the board or the water.

Cast. An entry where the body alignment is not parallel to the diving board at the point of contact with the water.

Checking. (1) The ability to compensate for any error in the dive that will cause coming out of the dive too early or too late. Proper checking (usually done with specific arm or head movements) often enables a perfect entry. (2) Making an underwater correction to give the optical illusion that the entry for the dive was perpendicular. Checking is also referred to as "saving a dive." This is an advanced maneuver.

Come-out. The proper time to cease rotation in somersaults or twists and prepare for entry.

Compulsory dive. Required dives in a competition. The committee running the event will specify which dives must be executed by all entrants. Usually, compulsory dives are those that have a limited degree of difficulty.

"Cross" position. Body position in which arms are held perpendicular to the shoulders. Also called the "T" position.

Cut the board. Leaving the board early, before it has provided its maximum amount of spring.

Degree of difficulty. A comparative system of rating the difficulty required to execute a dive. Each dive is assigned a numerical equivalant. The simpler dives possess low numbers, more difficult maneuvers have high designations.

Drop on dive. The height at which the diver finishes his

143

machinations and prepares for entry.

Duraflex diving board. The only aluminum springboard approved by F.I.N.A. for international meets. Invented and manufactured by Ray Rude of Arcadia Air Products.

Entering short. Making a dive entry with the body at an angle less than perpendicular (90-degree) to the water.

Fancy diving. Formal name for the sport of diving. Intricate in-air maneuvers culminating with a graceful entry into the water are the basis of the sport.

F.I.N.A. The Federation International Natation Association. The organization that puts out guidelines for the swimming and diving competitions held in the Olympics. All countries that compete in the Olympics are members of F.I.N.A.

Flange. The art of pressing forward on armstand dives with arms straight and elbows locked, as the body and shoulders are pushed away from the edge of the tower. This aids the diver achieving a proper leg-and-body position for the dive.

Forward dives. Dives in which the diver approaches the end of the board in a forward direction and takes off in a forward line to the water.

Forward dive straight. A basic forward dive in which the body position is straight, with arms out to the side in a "T," or "cross" position. Synonymous with the swan dive.

Forward flip. See "Forward somersault."

Forward somersault. A forward dive in which the body

makes an in-air rotation of 360 degrees.

Forward takeoff. The on-the-diving-board maneuvers prior to a forward dive. These may include a stepped takeoff, a hurdle, etc. All movements are made with the body facing toward the water.

Fosbury flop. Invented by high jumper Dick Fosbury. In this maneuver, the head and shoulders are first brought over the crossbar, with the legs then coming up to clear the bar. This body position is quite adaptable to executing reverse dives.

Free position. Applies to twisting dives where the diver has the option of executing the somersaults in tuck, pike, or layout position, after completing his twists.

Front somersault tuck. A forward somersault dive done in the tuck position.

Fulcrum. A movable bar on the diving board that controls the board's degree of flexibility. When the fulcrum is set to the back, the board will bend slower and softer. The fulcrum placed forward will create less leverage, hence the board will be stiffer and quicker.

Gainer. An old term for the reverse dive. The dive is also referred to as a "Mohlberg."

Going over. Entering "long" on a dive. Going over and beyond the 90-degree entry-angle to the water.

Hurdle. Segment at the end of the approach where the diver goes from a position on one foot into a two-foot jump from the end of the board.

Hurdle leg. The leg that comes up on the hurdle to initiate the two-foot jump off the board. The leg already planted on the board is known as the pressing leg, or power leg.

Hurdle step. The final step on the approach prior to the actual dive. The step can be taken with either the right or the left foot. It will carry the diver to the end of the board, in preparation for bringing down the hurdle leg and planting both feet in position for the takeoff.

Inward dive. A dive in which the diver positions himself with his back facing the water; the rotation is toward the end of the board, into the water.

Jackknife position. Old term for the pike position.

Kicking leg. Same as the "hurdle leg" when referring to springboard dive. On the platform, it is the takeoff leg on running reverse dives.

Kick-out. The leg extension in tuck position that serves to stop rotation.

Kip. A gymnastic term used to describe flipping up to one's feet from a position on one's back by quickly arching the back, springing the hands off the floor, and flexing the head forward to enable a landing on one's feet. Kip is employed to push off on armstand dives.

Leg snap. Quick extension of the bent knees while in the hurdle from the board. This, in combination with a forceful ankle snap, provides a powerful takeoff.

Maxiflex diving board. Springboard similar to the Duraflex model, only it is tapered to a greater degree at the base and tip. This makes it lighter and more flexible, with a slower and softer feel.

Metatarsals. The "pad" portion of the foot. The point at

which the toes are attached.

Mohlberg. See "Gainer."

Olympic-type pool. A pool that is a minimum of twelve feet deep under the three-meter diving board, and seventeen feet deep under the ten-meter board. The required pool length is fifty meters.

One-meter springboard. A springboard positioned one meter above the water level, as measured from the top of the board.

Optional dives. Dives selected by the diver for use in a competition. These dives may be of any degree of difficulty.

Peripheral vision. The field of vision beyond the central focal point.

Pike position. A position in which the diver bends at the waist and clutches his outstretched legs with his hands at a point below or under the knees.

Platform. Also known as a tower. A stationary diving surface located at varying heights above water level. This diving surface provides no spring.

Platform diving. Also known as tower diving. A division of the sport in which a diver catapults himself off the platform (with the only spring to achieve altitude coming from leg power) to execute various dives.

Preliminary competition. The first round of a diving competition, in which all divers participate. The divers with the highest marks in this segment advance to the semifinal and final rounds.

Press. The act of pressing, or pushing, the feet into the

147

diving board to gain maximum flex. Coordinated arm movement adds to the degree of flex.

Reverse dive. A dive in which the diver approaches the end of the board in a forward direction, then, upon takeoff, changes direction (while jumping a safe distance from the board) to rotate toward the board. All springboard takeoffs for this dive must be from both feet.

Rip entry. An entry into the water that creates as little a splash as possible. Rip entries aid in achieving high scores.

Running reverse flip. See "Running reverse somersault."

Running reverse somersault. A reverse somersault dive begun from a forward takeoff.

Runway. That portion of the diving board used by the diver to make his approach.

Seat drop. A method of piking out of a twisting dive. The diver positions his extended legs with ankles and toes pointed directly under the body. It should seem as if the diver will not be landing on the seat of his pants.

Sinusitis. Infection of the sinuses.

Skim-off. A method used in running takeoffs from the platform. Rather than employing a high hurdle, the diver takes a low step prior to the two-foot takeoff.

Somersault. Rotating the body 360 degrees while in the air. Somersault dives are done in forward, reverse, back, and inward positions.

Space orientation. The ability to have your brain (balance center) tell you how many somersaults and twists you have completed.

Spotting. (1) Actually using your eyes during a somersault to establish your position in relation to the water and the board, as well as to count the number of somersaults completed. With increased experience, "space orientation" will provide this knowledge with eyes closed. (2) Having a coach guide you with his hands or a spotting belt to aid in learning various dives, mainly somersaults and twists.

Spotting belt. A safety belt attached to the rigging of a trampoline. The other end of the belt is placed around the diver to prevent injuries while practicing somersaults and flips.

Split tuck. A tuck position in which the diver spreads his knees and feet. It is considered improper form and will cost points when done in competition.

Spreadeagle position. A "cross," or "T," position.

Springboard. The board used by divers to literally "spring" them into the air for their dives. It is placed at varying heights above water level.

Standing takeoff. Taking off from a springboard or platform without implementing a hurdle.

Step-off. Measuring your strides so you will know the exact point from which you will be taking off.

Stepped takeoff. The actual process of walking to the end of the diving board for the takeoff.

Straight position. A diving position in which there is no bend in any part of the body from the toes to the outstretched hands.

Swimmer's ear. Usually an external infection of the ear canal (skin lining).

Ten-point dive. The highest score one can receive for a dive. A perfect dive.

"T" position. See "Cross position."

Tuck position. A diving position in which the diver rolls himself into a tight ball by bringing his legs and thighs up to his chest and holding them together with his hands.

Twisters. See "Twisting dives."

Twisting dives. Dives in which the diver pirouettes 180 or 360 degrees one or more times.

Visual orientation. Using the eyes to count flips as well as establish location in relation to board and water.

Voluntary dives. See "Optional dives."

Dr. Sammy Lee

Dr. Sammy Lee is one of the foremost authorities on diving in the United States. In 1948 he captured a gold medal in platform diving and a bronze in the springboard competition at the Olympic Games in London; in 1952 he became the first man to win back-to-back Olympic high diving titles by earning another gold medal for platform diving in Helsinki. Dr. Lee is also the first man to coach a diver to back-to-back Olympic victories (Bob Webster, 1960 and 1964). He now coaches Greg Louganis, the youngest silver medalist in the history of Olympic diving. Dr. Lee practices medicine in southern California, where he resides with his wife. He is the father of two children.